Yorkshire Place-Names

by

William Thurlow

Dalesman Books

1979

The Dalesman Publishing Company Ltd.,
Clapham (via Lancaster), North Yorkshire

First published 1979

ISBN: 0 85206 544 2

Printed by Herald Rusholmes Printers (Westminster Press Ltd.), York.

Contents

Cover photograph by the author.

Back cover design and map by Barbara Yates.

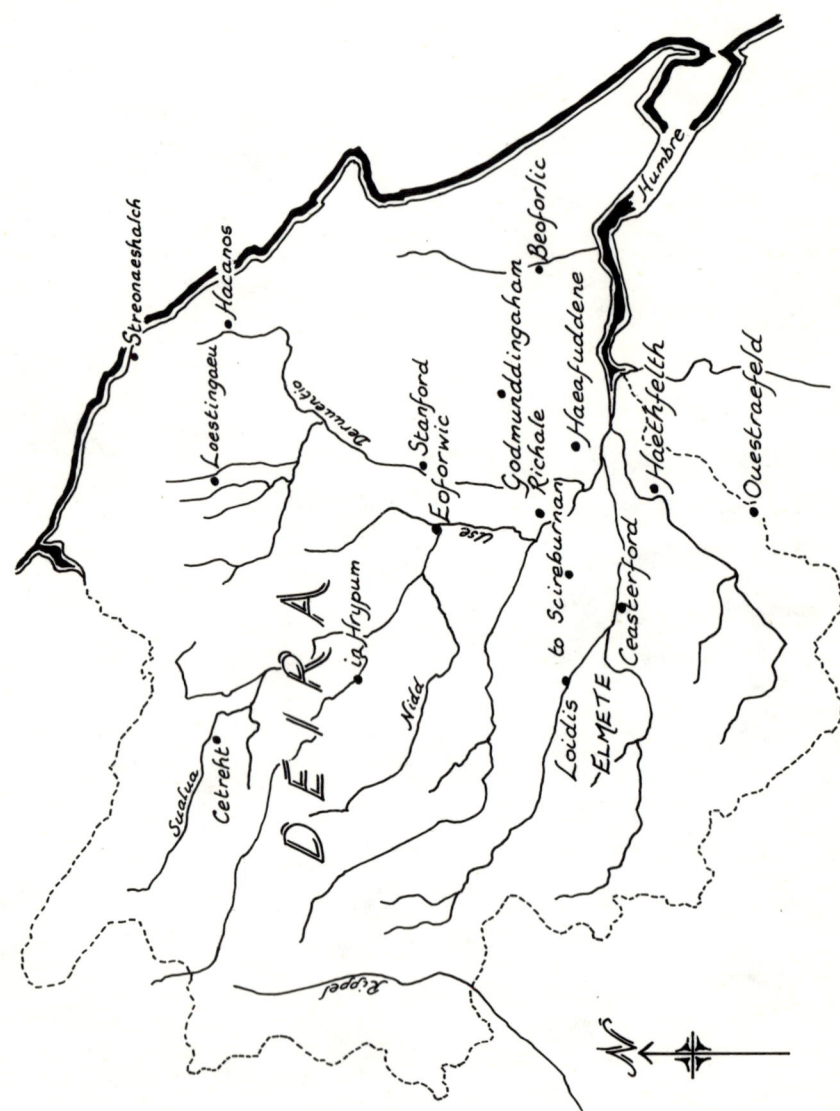

Fig. 1. Anglian Yorkshire: Place-names having a recorded Anglo-Saxon form.

Foreword

THIS book is an introduction to the subject of Yorkshire place-names, which, as I hope, will encourage the reader to study further. In such a short survey I have been unable to deal with more than a limited number of place-names, but have tried to include the more important and interesting ones. For the most part it has not been possible to give anything more than a bare explanation of each name included. As a Yorkshireman, I make no apology for basing the survey on the Yorkshire of the Ridings, and not on the county as it exists today.

Inevitably this book owes much to the efforts of the various eminent scholars who have made so many important contributions to English place-name studies. In particular I am very much indebted to the volumes on Yorkshire place-names by Professor A. H. Smith in the English Place-Name Society Survey, and I wish to thank Professor Kenneth Cameron, Honorary Director of the Survey, for his courtesy in giving me permission to make use of the material contained therein.

ABBREVIATIONS

M.E.	— Middle English.
Mod.E.	— Modern English.
O.Dan.	— Old Danish.
O.E.	— Old English (Anglo-Saxon).
O.E.Scand.	— Old East Scandinavian.
O.N.	— Old Norse (Old Icelandic forms of Old West Scandinavian).
O.Nb.	— Old Northumbrian dialect of Old English.
O.Fr.	— Old French.
O.Ir.	— Old Irish.
O.W.Scand.	— Old West Scandinavian.
O.Welsh	— Old Welsh.
Y.E.	— East Riding of Yorkshire.
Y.N.	— North Riding of Yorkshire.
Y.W.	— West Riding of Yorkshire.
*	— A postulated or reconstructed form.

1. Introductory

FROM the earliest times, wherever he has settled, man has given human significance to the principal physical features of his environment. By giving an individual name to neighbouring farms and villages, and hills, valleys, streams and woods in the locality, the members of a community were able to identify them precisely to their common advantage. Such place-names had to be sufficiently descriptive to make identification easy, and yet simple enough to become generally accepted by the community. In course of time the more important of these place-names would begin to have a wider currency and so become known to more distant settlements. Although the names so given may have an immense variety, they fall into four broad classes: folk-names, habitation-names, nature-names and names given in commemoration of a person or an event.

Folk-names are names originally given to a tribe or people, which by a transfer of meaning come to denote the place in which they live. Thus Prussia and Sweden mean 'land of the Prussians' and 'land of the Swedes' respectively. In England Essex, Middlesex and Sussex are names similarly derived from the people inhabiting those places, namely the East, Middle and South Saxons respectively. Such place-names arose when migratory groups began to settle in a particular locality. In Yorkshire a place-name of this type is Ripon, which is derived from the name of an Anglian tribe called the Hrype.

Habitation-names, which form the most important class of English place-names, are names describing inhabited places, in other words: homesteads, farms, hamlets, villages and towns. Nature-names, also an important class, are names describing topographical features, and are also often used to denote inhabited places. Place-names commemorating a person or an event are commonly found in the U.S.A. and the older Commonwealth countries, for example Washington, Independence, Adelaide, Wellington, Vancouver, etcetera. In England many habitation- and nature-names incorporate personal names, but since these normally refer to unidentified people, they are not usually regarded as commemorative names.

Sometimes a single appellative was used as a habitation-name. Thus O.E. *wic*, meaning 'a farm', especially 'a dairy-farm', later 'a village', occurs as Wyke. Such a place-name, and others like Croft, Thorpe, and the like, formed in a similar way from a single word or element, are called simplex names. To make for more precise identification, however, two or more elements were combined together to form a compound place-name, such as Appletreewick 'dairy-farm near an apple-tree', Seacroft 'enclosure by a marsh' or Austhorpe 'east outlying farmstead'. Similarly, a nature-name, consisting of a single element, often denoted a particular place, and so we have place-names like Hurst 'wood', Cliffe 'cliff', Clough 'ravine' and Well 'spring, stream'. As with habitation-names, however, it is more usual to find two or more elements in combination, as in Hazlewood 'hazel wood', Birkenshaw 'birch wood' and Thornbrough 'thorn hill'. Other ways in which place-names are formed are described in Chapter 5.

The interpretation of some place-names presents no difficulties. The meaning of such names as Harthill, Stonebeck and Foxholes, for example, is self-evident, while that of a place-name like Bradford ('broad ford') may easily be deduced. On the other hand some place-names whose meaning is apparently quite clear may mean something very different: the first element of Featherstone is not 'feather' but O.E. *feother* 'four' and the place has acquired its name from a cromlech[1] in the vicinity; Fryup has nothing to do with culinary activities, but is derived from O.E. 'Friga', a woman's name, and *hop* 'a small valley'; and Follifoot has no connection with 'folly' or 'foot' but means 'the place of a horse-fight', so named because the Scandinavians were addicted to this form of sport. Many place-names, like Scholes, Drax, Hunslet and Cracoe, for example, offer no clue as to their meaning, which seems quite obscure. In the majority of cases, in fact, place-names in their modern form are either misleading or unintelligible.

Difficulties of interpretation arise because most English place-names are so ancient. Some that still survive are Celtic or even pre-Celtic, although most are of English origin, with a high proportion of Scandinavian origin or affected by Scandinavian influence in those parts of England where the Viking invaders settled, and were mainly established between the sixth and eleventh centuries. Although this period is very remote and many details of its history are obscure and open to conjecture, it had an important bearing on the course of later English history. It was during this period before the Norman Conquest that England assumed its characteristic pattern: the English emerged as its dominant people; the country was unified under a monarchy; Christianity became accepted as its religion; and English became firmly established as its language.

The development of the English language during the course of centuries has had an important influence on the development of English place-names. The language spoken by the Anglo-Saxon invaders, usually now called Old English rather than Anglo-Saxon, was a branch of West Germanic, which went back via Primitive Germanic to its parent language, Indo-European. Old English was an inflected language, with nouns of masculine, feminine and neuter gender, in strong and weak classes, and

---

[1] Cromlech is a structure of prehistoric age consisting of a large flat unhewn stone resting horizontally on three or more stones set upright.

with distinctive nominative, accusative, genitive and dative case-endings in the singular and plural, while adjectives were declined according to class, and there were weak and strong verbs. Three main Old English dialects emerged during the period of the English settlement: West Saxon, Kentish and Anglian, the last named being further subdivided into Northumbrian and Mercian.

The English language was strongly influenced by Scandinavian as a result of the Viking invasions during the ninth and tenth centuries, and after the Norman Conquest there was also considerable French influence. During the Middle Ages as Old English developed into Middle English, loss of inflexions and gender occurred. With the ascendancy of the East Midland dialect over other English dialects as it developed into the standard language and with the changes of pronunciation known as the Great Vowel Shift, English began to assume its modern recognisable form.

Since place-names have been subject to the same sound changes and influences that have affected the language itself, they have changed their form considerably since they were first established. The development of a place-name like York provides an example. In Celtic times York was called *Eburacon*, derived either from a personal-name *Eburos* or *eburos* 'a yew-tree'. The geographer Ptolemy, writing in A.D. 150, shows it as a Greek form *Eborakon*, and in late Latin it was Eboracum. During the period of English settlement *Ebor-* was replaced by O.E. *eofor* 'a boar' and the suffix *-acum* by O.E. *wic* 'village'. The form of the place-name became *Iorvik*, later *Iork*, through Scandinavian influence after the city was captured by the Danes in the ninth century, and finally took its modern form, York, in the thirteenth century.

Since place-names have undergone such radical changes of form and pronunciation, a satisfactory explanation of their meaning depends upon the evidence provided by early spellings. It is only when all the spellings of a place-name from the available documentary evidence over the course of centuries have been collected and arranged in chronological order, after their identity and reliability have been established, that its development may be seen and the work of interpretation can begin. The trained philologist then applies specialised techniques, using his linguistic and topographical knowledge and general experience, to discover its derivation.

The earliest documents relating to English place-names are the *Geography* of Ptolemy, mentioned above, the fourth century *Antonine Itinerary* and the seventh century *Cosmography* by an unknown author, and these are invaluable for details of Romano-British names. The Venerable Bede's *History of the English Church and People*, although written in Latin, is another source of early forms. Also written in Latin are the charters of the Old English period, most of which, however, were copied after the Norman Conquest and are not always accurate copies of the originals. An important historical document, the *Anglo-Saxon Chronicle*, written in Old English, also contains invaluable references. But the records of the Old English period show comparatively few place-names, and the most important single source is the eleventh-century *Domesday Book*, although it was compiled by Norman scribes who were unfamiliar with the sounds of Old English. These early basic documents are supplemented during the Middle English period by many official records relating to taxation, grants, court proceedings, etcetera, and much local evidence in the form of cartularies[1] of abbeys, estate records and manorial rolls, and in later years by estate plans, surveys of land, enclosure awards and maps.

Even with an extensive collection of early forms arranged in chronological sequence, many difficulties of interpretation may arise. The available evidence may still be incomplete or inaccurate, and it has to be borne in mind that the earliest forms may possibly be corrupt, and a later form may even represent a true earlier form. The enquiry may be complicated because the early spellings show dialectal variation or may show the influence of another language, even to the extent of being hybrid forms which include elements from different languages. Sometimes a place-name may have been influenced by folk or popular etymology, that is by an alteration to its form to make it more easily understood (an instance of this in language generally is the word *sparrowgrass* for *asparagus*). Thus, in the example of York given previously, the English substituted the word *eofor* 'boar' and *wic* 'village', which had significance for them, for *Ebor-* and *-acum*, which they found quite meaningless.

Confusion may arise, too, where elements which are different in meaning, develop similarly in form. Thus O.E. *beorg* 'hill' and O.E. *burh* 'fortified place' may both develop into the modern form *-borough*. It is possible, too, that although the derivation of a place-name may be found, the exact significance of its constituent elements may not be known or their meaning may have changed. O.E. *feld* provides an example of the latter: in the Old English period it was generally used in the sense of 'an open stretch of country' and then 'cultivated land'; by the Middle Ages it had come to mean 'the common field'; and it was only after the Black Death, when enclosures began to be made, that it first acquired the meaning 'field'.

Where there appears to be no written evidence of the word from which the place-name seems to have arisen, and yet several place-names point back to that word, the investigator may make the assumption that it existed and suggest a form for it. Such reconstructed forms are prefixed by an * in this book. Since extant Old English literature is not extensive, the fact that a word does not occur therein does not necessarily mean that it did not exist, especially if there is clear evidence of the existence of a cognate[2] word in related languages. Thus there is a good deal of evidence by the frequency of place-names in *-royd*, for example Royd(s), Ackroyd, Boothroyd, Oldroyd, and so on, for the existence of O.E. *rod* 'clearing'; and from place-names such as Ridding(s) (4), Riding(s) (3), (The) Ruddings, etcetera, we may suppose the existence of *rydding, also meaning 'clearing'.

---

[1] Cartullaries are a collection of records or registers.
[2] Cognate means a word from the same linguistic family.

The topography of a place may also be relevant, and an examination of a site may afford a clue to the explanation of a place-name. The bends of the River Hodder near Bowland confirm that the place-name is derived from O.E. *bogena-land* and means 'land by the bow or bends of the river'. It must be remembered, however, that many topographical changes have occurred since early times; marshes have been drained, moorland has been reclaimed, woodland has been cleared and rivers have changed their course. The modern pronunciation of a place-name may be of importance too, especially where there have been changes of spelling to obscure the original form. A knowledge of local history may also be invaluable, especially where feudal affixes have been added to older place-names.

The study of etymology of place-names is of some fascination to those who are curious about the past. But it is more than an interesting intellectual exercise; it is of importance for its bearing on the problem of history, especially in periods when written records are scanty or non-existent. Place-names studies have helped, along with complementary studies in archaeology, to throw a good deal of light on what happened in England between the departure of the Romans and the Norman Conquest. In particular they provide invaluable knowledge of the patterns of Anglo-Saxon and Scandinavian settlement, and much important information about religion, industry, agriculture, commerce and social conditions during this early period.

They also have a bearing on linguistic studies. They provide knowledge of unrecorded English words, both with and without cognate words in related languages. The distribution of place-names is of importance, too, for a knowledge of the date and extent of sound changes, particularly as they affect dialects. The different development of O.E. *wella* 'well, spring' provides an illustration: Anglian and Kentish *wella* is found as Well, Rothwell, Shadwell, Wells, etcetera; the West Saxon form *wiella* became either *wille* as in Wilton, or *wulle*, as in Woolcombe, Woolley, and the like; and Mercian *waelle* became *walle*, as in Colwall and Etwall. By plotting the distribution of place-names incorporating elements that develop differently, the extent of sound changes may be established and dialect boundaries fixed.

The place-names of Yorkshire are of particular historical and linguistic importance. During the period between the end of Roman rule and the Norman Conquest, the area we now know as Yorkshire was subjected to a momentous political and social transformation. First a Celtic kingdom emerged within its boundaries, to be followed by an extensive, permanent settlement by the English, and then by further settlements, first by Danes and then by Norwegians, who were powerful enough to found and to hold for a time a Scandinavian kingdom of York. The county's varied and turbulent history during these centuries is reflected in the richness and diversity of its place-names. The reader should find their study both interesting and rewarding.

10

2. The Celtic Element

DURING the Roman occupation of Britain, most of Yorkshire was situated in the civil zone, with its northerly parts and the central parts of the Pennines to the west within the military zone. York, the capital of Lower Britain, was an important military base for the forces along Hadrian's Wall, with a large *colonia* or settlement of time-expired Roman soldiers. There were Roman stations at Doncaster, Castleford, Catterick, Malton, and perhaps at Tadcaster, with signal stations on the coast during the late Roman period, while communications were assured by a network of Roman roads. The native population consisted of the large tribe of Brigantes, who occupied much of northern England and had their capital at Aldborough (*Isurium Brigantum*), near Boroughbridge, and the Parisii, who occupied the East Riding and had their tribal capital at Brough-on-Humber (*Petuaria*).

Much of Yorkshire, particularly the hilly country to the west, seems to have been sparsely populated, and the native population, except for the upper classes, who were most probably bilingual, spoke British. The Celtic language, from which British was descended, had at a very early date split into two branches, one of which, Goidelic, was the language from which Irish, Scots and Manx Gaelic developed, and the other, Gallo-Brittonic, from which Gaulish, as well as British, developed. At a later stage, Welsh, Cornish and Breton developed from British.

During the third century A.D. Saxon pirates began to raid the coasts of Britain, and it was to provide a system of warning against their raids that Roman signal stations were built at Whitby and Scarborough and other places on the north-east coast. There may possibly have been some settlements by Saxons in Yorkshire even while Britain was occupied by the Romans, who used them as mercenaries against the Picts. After the Roman legions were withdrawn from Britain during the early part of the fifth century, groups of Anglo-Saxon invaders began to penetrate inland from the east coast and found settlements, and ultimately, by about A.D. 700, had occupied the whole of England except Cornwall.

Yorkshire was not completely overrun until after the fall of the British kingdom of Elmet, which occurred some time after 616. This kingdom probably comprised the land between the rivers Aire and Wharfe, with its eastern boundary situated somewhere near the present A1, defences to the north-east being provided by the earthworks at Becca Banks at Aberford. The district of Craven may also have had some form of organised British community, while there is evidence of the survival of an enclave of Britons on the North Yorkshire Moors.

Although British resistance continued for many years, in the end the Anglo-Saxon settlement was complete, and so thorough that only a handful of Celtic words survive in the English language. The reason for this is not clear. The possibility exists, although the theory is generally discounted, that a wholesale massacre of the native population occurred. It seems more probable that because of the inferior status of the Britons little intermarriage took place and the Celtic language gradually died out. Whatever the reason the influence of Celtic on the English language was inconsiderable.

There are, however, many place-names of Celtic origin in England, although their number and distribution vary according to locality. Professor Kenneth Jackson in *Language and History in Early Britain* has divided England into three principal areas, based on the distribution of river-names, which are generally less influenced by changes than other place-names. In the first area, which runs roughly east of a line from the Yorkshire Wolds to Southampton, the names of the principal rivers, some topographical features and some towns are Celtic. In the second area, which runs east of the Cumbrian and Lancashire border, then through Chester to the Bristol Channel, and to the English Channel east of Somerset and Dorset, Celtic survivals, which also include the names of minor rivers, are more numerous. And in the third area, which includes Cumbria and Lancashire, the Welsh Marches and south-west England, Celtic names are quite common. In Wales, except for small pockets where English influence was strong, Celtic names are usual. These areas tend to coincide with the progress of the Anglo-Saxon settlement: the first area coincides with the early settlements in eastern parts; the second that of further advance after consolidation; and the third that of late settlement after England was finally conquered.

In that part of the first area lying in Yorkshire, mainly consisting of the East Riding, the names of Humber, Derwent and perhaps Ouse are Celtic in origin, together with York, and the name of the Anglian kingdom of Deira. In the rest of Yorkshire, which lies in the second area, most of the river-names are of Celtic origin, but few Celtic place-names have survived, and even in Elmet itself, which includes Leeds and its neighbourhood, their concentration is not high. It may be that the region was thinly populated, and few place-names existed. In other areas, such as the Vale of York, the south-east and the north-west, the scarcity of Celtic survivals may be the result of the intensive Scandinavian settlement that took place in these parts in the ninth and tenth centuries.

That the Celtic names of the principal rivers of Yorkshire have mainly survived is not surprising. These are natural features that extend over a distance and are common to various communities. The Anglo-Saxon invaders, who used the rivers to penetrate inland, would no doubt have

12

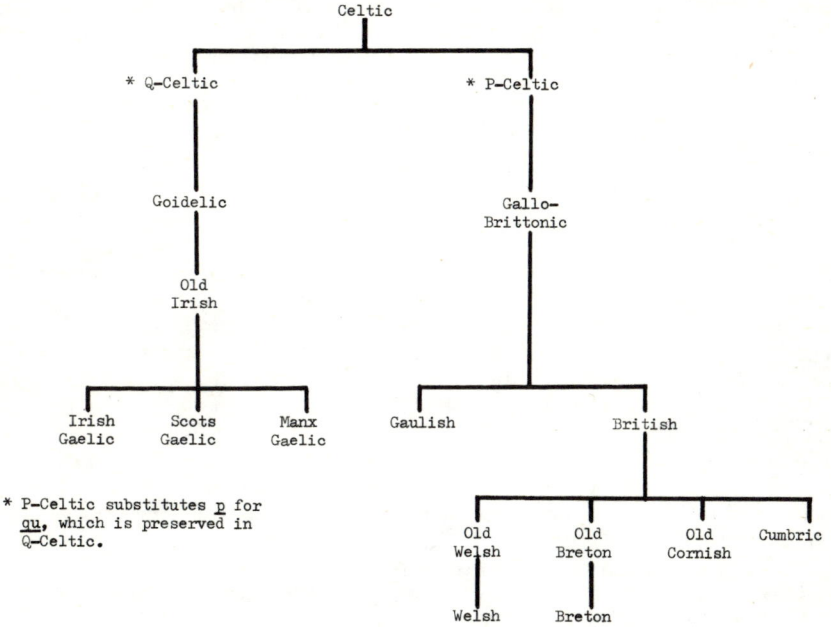

Fig. 2: The Celtic Languages

soon learned their names from the native population, quickly accepted them, and then simply continued to use them.

Several Yorkshire river-names are derived from British roots meaning 'water' or 'river': Esk from the British *Isca* is identical with Exe and Usk found elsewhere; Rother is from a prefix *ro-* and *dubro-* 'water' and probably means 'chief river'; Rye, possibly from a word cognate with Latin *rivus* 'stream' also gives its name to Riccal, meaning 'calf of' or 'little Rye'; Seven may be from the same root as Somme in France; Don is probably from British **dana*, from a root **dan-*; and Ouse may be from a base **udso*.

Some river-names are descriptive: names referring to colour are Dove and Tame, meaning 'dark'; and Nidd, which gives its name to the village of Nidd, is probably derived from a root meaning 'brilliant'. Several names refer to the turbulence of the water: Tees may be derived from a word meaning 'surging'; Calder from a word meaning 'violent'; Aire may be from the British **Isara* 'strong river' and Ure may be from a connected word **Isura*, from which O.E. *Ior* developed; Colne may mean 'roaring'; and Laver is from **labaro-* 'talkative' and hence 'murmuring'.

On the other hand, Leven, which is identical with Llyfni and Llynfi in Wales, means 'smooth, placid' and Hodder means 'peaceful'. Derwent,

13

identical with Darent, Dart and Darwen, is a river-name derived from the British *derva* 'oak' and probably means 'river lined with oaks'. In Cover there is a reference to the course of the river, the first element being a word meaning 'hollow' or 'ravine'. Kyle means 'narrow' and Wharfe means 'winding river'. Crimple Beck, an affluent[1] of the Nidd, is from a word which corresponds to Welsh *crwn* 'crooked'. In Humber, of which there are several examples in England, and Lune, we have references to the quality of the water itself, such as 'good' or 'health-giving'. The meaning of Went is obscure, but it may be of British origin. It is to be noted that the etymology of several of the river-names dealt with so far, in particular, Aire, Ouse, Tees and Ure, is by no means certain, and the possibility exists that some of them may even be of pre-Celtic origin.

The names of two well-known Yorkshire mountains are derived from Celtic. Penyghent is from the British *penno-* 'hill', the final element being obscure. Penhill, with the same first element, is a tautological compound and literally means 'hill-hill'. The most likely explanation of the form is that the Angles did not know the meaning of Pen- when they added the suffix. In Pendle Hill the explanatory O.E. *hyll* has even been added twice. It is to be noted, however, that the name Pennines is not derived from *penno-* and is not in fact very ancient; it first appears in an eighteenth century forgery of a work supposedly by Richard of Cirencester, but the origin of the word is not known. The Chevin, near Otley, is another example of a Celtic hill-name, being derived from O.Welsh *cefn* 'ridge'.

Elmet, preserved in Barwick in Elmet and Sherburn in Elmet, is most certainly British, although its etymology is uncertain. Craven, which gives its name to a district, may be derived from a British word meaning 'garlic' although the reason for this is obscure. *Deira*, the name of the Anglian kingdom that comprised Yorkshire, is probably from the British *dobriu* and may mean 'a land where there are many rivers'.

Of town place-names of Celtic origin, the name York has been dealt with in Chapter 1. Leeds, which may have been the capital of the kingdom of Elmet, is an interesting but difficult name. Bede refers to Leeds as *in regione (quae vocatur) Loidis*, and the place-name is probably derived from British *Lat-*, which Professor Smith in *The Place-Names of the West Riding* suggests may have been the former name of the River Aire, then a folk-name, and ultimately the name of a district. Nearby Ledsham and Ledston both mean 'homestead belonging to Leeds'. Doncaster and Dewsbury have Old English final elements, the former with *ceaster* meaning 'fortification on the River Don', and the latter, consisting of a Welsh personal name 'Dewi' combined with *burh*, also meaning 'fortification'. There is a possibility that Ilkley developed from *Olicana*, the name of the Roman station there, the first element being from a British root and the second element O.E. *leah* 'clearing', although it has been suggested that the first element is derived from the O.E. personal-name

---

[1] Affluent is a tributary stream.

'Ylla'. The first element of Penistone is the British *penno- 'hill', with the suffix O.E. ing and the final element O.E. tun 'homestead'. Dent is another British name, perhaps derived from a word cognate with O.Ir. dinn 'a hill'. Catterick, where a Roman station was situated, may have originally come from a British word *catar- (compare this with the Welsh cader), meaning 'hill-fort'. The Romans took the British name to be from Latin cataracta 'waterfall' and so it appears as Cataractone in the Antonine Itinerary.

There are a few other names of Celtic origin in Yorkshire. Ecclesall, Ecclesfield, Eccleshill and Exley, all incorporating the British *eclesia 'church', are interesting in that they may indicate the existence of Christian churches in these places at the time of the Anglo-Saxon invasions. Crigglestone, from O.E. cryc-hyll, the first element of which contains O.Welsh cruc 'hill', is another place-name of the 'hill-hill' type. Roos and Rossington may be from O.Welsh ros 'moor', the latter also with O.E. ing and tun, while Chevet, like Chevin, is connected with cefn 'ridge'. Catterton is a name from the British *cateira 'seat', borrowed from Latin cathedra. Place-names compounded with O.E. personal names of Welsh origin are Campsall 'Cam' with O.E. halh 'nook of land', Camblesforth 'Camela' with O.E. ford 'ford' and Cumberworth 'Cumbra' with O.E. worth 'clearing'.

Dacre may have been the original name of Darley Beck and possibly means 'trickling stream'. Alne is another place-name which was originally a river name, and probably referred to the Kyle, as also was Leeming, which is derived from the British *lemanio, meaning 'elm'. Glaisdale contains a first element corresponding to Welsh glas 'blue, grey', and Crayke, built on a steep hill, is from the British *krakjo 'a rock'.

There are also several place-names in Yorkshire which contain O.E. walh, meaning 'Welshman, foreigner, serf'. Such names are Walton (3) with O.E. tun, Walshford with O.E. ford, Walburn with O.E. burna 'stream' and Walden with O.E. denu 'valley'. In addition there is the place-name Wales 'the Welshmen', formed from the nominative plural of walh. These names may all indicate isolated villages still inhabited by Britons after the Anglian settlement. On the other hand since the word walh also means 'serf', they may simply have referred to villages where serfs lived. Of course, most serfs were probably Britons when these place-names were first established.

3.   The English Element

THE Angles, Saxons and Jutes who invaded and settled in England after the departure of the Romans belonged to the Germanic people. The Angles came from the Danish mainland, the Saxons from north-west Germany and the Jutes, about whom there is much speculation, probably came from an area to the south of the Saxons. Although described as Angles, Saxons and Jutes, they spoke the same language, English, and regarded themselves as belonging to one people—*Angel-cynn* 'the English people'. In the first stages of settlement the invaders probably consisted of small tribal groups, which soon coalesced to form larger organised units, and the process so continued until by the early eighth century England consisted of seven kingdoms, the Heptarchy. In the North Northumbria, which had been formed from the early kingdoms of Bernicia, comprising Northumberland, and Deira, comprising most of Yorkshire, had some ascendancy over the other English kingdoms during the seventh century; in the eighth century Mercia was the dominant kingdom; and then Wessex in the ninth century.

The invasion and settlement of Yorkshire was made by the Angles, who sailed up the estuary of the Humber, and then along the Ouse and Derwent. They made early settlements near Driffield, in Holderness and in the Vale of Pickering. From the neighbourhood of Malton they penetrated to the Vale of York, where their westward movement was impeded by the resistance of the British kingdom of Elmet, and then advanced northwards, probably along the belt of magnesium limestone by the A1, up to the Tees, and westwards into the lower reaches of Wensleydale. With the victory of Aethelfrith of Bernicia over the British at Chester in 616 and the subjugation of Elmet some time afterwards, the way was clear for the settlement of the rest of Yorkshire, which was probably completed during the seventh century. It was not, of course, until after the Scandinavian settlement that the county became an administrative unit and was actually called Yorkshire, and that the further division into Ridings took place. Administrative units that were smaller than a county were also given the name 'shire', and so in Yorkshire we have such names as Hallamshire, Mashamshire and Richmondshire.

During the early English period Northumbrian developed as the dialect spoken by the inhabitants of Yorkshire, although there was some penetration by Mercians from the south, perhaps as a result of the military struggle between Northumbria and Mercia during the eighth century,

16

and some Yorkshire place-names show characteristics of the Mercian dialect. The linguistic boundary between Mercia and Northumbria was approximately along the line of the River Wharfe.

The first elements of the place-names Markenfield and Markington may mean 'Mercians', and if so, these places may well represent the most northerly parts reached by Mercians penetrating south Yorkshire. There is a possibility, however, that these place-names mean 'boundary dwellers' and refer to the early settlement of a people called the Hrype, whose name survives in Ripon. The first element of Ripley may also refer to the Hrype, and it has even been suggested that there were two groups of this people, one passing along the Ouse to Ripon, and the other along the Trent to found a settlement at Repton in Derbyshire. The possibility that there were Saxons settling in Yorkshire among the Angles is suggested by the place-name Saxton 'the Saxons' village', although the first element may have been a personal name. Ferry Fryston and Monk Fryston, 'the village of the Frisians', together with Frizinghall, suggest the presence of Frisians alongside the Angles, and since these peoples lived in neighbouring areas on the Continent and the Frisians were famous seafarers, such an explanation seems reasonable.

At this point, in dealing with early settlement, we are concerned with the complex problem of what are termed place-names in *-ingas*. The plural form, *-ingas*, when added to a personal name, was used in the sense of 'the people of', and the folk-name so formed was transferred to the name of the place where the people settled. In Yorkshire we have place-names taken from such folk-names as Fitling '(the settlement of) Fitela and his people' and Pickering '(the settlement of) Picer and his people'. Other place-names of this type are Fylingdales, Gembling, Gilling (2), Kiplin, Leavening and East and West Lilling. These group names are also found in the genitive plural, *-inga-*, combined with other elements, such as *ham*, *leah* and *tun*. Thus we have, among others, Barningham 'homestead of Beorna and his people', Lastingham 'homestead of Last and his people', Killinghall 'the nook of land of Cylla's people' and Whashton 'homestead of Hwassa and his people'.

The etymology of *-ingas* names presents many difficulties. It is not always certain that the first element is derived from a personal name, and there is also the added complication that many place-names, which are apparently names in *-ingas*, are in reality formed from the connective particle *ing*, compounded with other elements, but mainly *tun*, and with a personal name used in the sense of 'associated with'. Thus Drighlington means 'farmstead associated with Dryhtel' and Illingworth 'enclosure associated with Illa'. The suffix *ing* was also used to form place-names such as Bowling (from O.E. *bolla* 'hollow') and Cowling (from O.E. **coll* 'hill'). Thus the mere presence of *ing* in a place-name does not necessarily mean that it is derived from a folk-name, and its etymology can only be found if there are sufficient early and reliable spellings. A list of names in *-ingas*, *-ingaham* and *-inga-* plus suffix, together with names in *ing* plus suffix, is given at the end of the chapter.

17

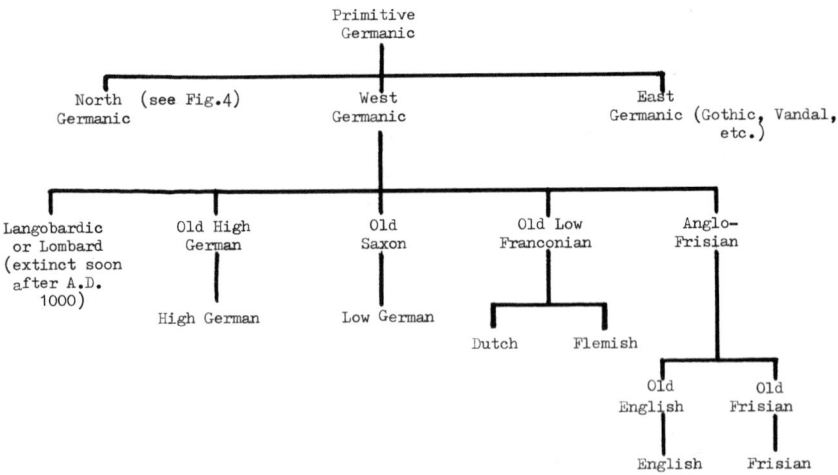

Fig. 3: The West Germanic Languages

For a long time it was believed that names in *-ingas* were related to actual migratory groups of Anglo-Saxons from the Continent and that names in *-ingaham* were formed at a slightly later period. On the basis of this theory, such names were very important in helping to define areas of early settlement. In the 1960s, however, serious doubts began to arise about its validity after comparisons between the distribution of such place-names and of pagan burial grounds in selected areas had been made and had shown little correspondence. Doubts have also arisen about the validity of other assumptions, namely that *-ingas* names are earlier than *-ingaham* names and even that habitation-names are earlier than nature-names. Perhaps further investigation may ultimately resolve many of the problems that have now arisen in connection with the chronology of place-names after the rejection of such theories of long-standing.

Although we have seen, most river-names in Yorkshire are of Celtic origin, there are a few English names. The Swale means 'rushing river' and the Ribble, like the Sheaf, means 'boundary stream'. Wiske 'meadow stream' takes its name from the meadows through which it flows during much of its course, while Balder has been formed from Baldersdale 'Baldhere's valley'. Idle, from O.E. *idel*, may possibly mean 'sluggish'. The Foss, a common river-name, means 'ditch', while Dearne may be derived from *dierne* 'hidden' and Wenning from *wann* 'dark'. Rivelin simply means 'rivulet'. O.E. *burna* 'stream' gives its name to the Burn, an affluent of the River Ure, and is the second element of Ryburn 'fierce' and Washburn, compounded with a personal-name 'Walc'.

By far the most common element in Yorkshire place-names, as in English place-names generally, is *tun*. It survived as a living element

18

from the early period of settlement to the post-Conquest period, and during that time changed its meaning from 'enclosure' to 'homestead', then to 'village', and finally to 'town'. It is fairly evenly distributed over most of Yorkshire, and after the Scandinavian invasions is found compounded with Scandinavian personal-names in place-names known as 'Grimston hybrids'. As we have seen in the previous chapter it is also found in a few place-names compounded with a Celtic first element.

Not found as a simplex name, and rarely found as a first element, as a second element *tun* is compounded with a variety of different types of significant words, generally with the meaning of 'farmstead' or 'village', although its precise meaning is not always known. Location is specified in place-names like Aston, Easton and Eston 'east', Norton *frequently* 'north', Sutton *frequently* 'south', Weston 'west' and Middleton 'middle'. There is a descriptive first element in Breighton 'bright', Grinton 'green', Kirkheaton 'high', Langton (3) 'long', Lepton and Litton 'on the slope', Mickleton 'large', Newton *frequently* 'new' and Oulton 'old'. Stockton on the Forest means 'enclosure with a stockade', Crofton 'enclosure with a croft' and Steeton (2) 'enclosure where there are tree-stumps'. A reference to products is made in Coulton '*tun* where charcoal is burnt'. Bempton is 'a farmstead by a tree' and East and West Rounton, Shafton and Stapleton (2) mean 'farmstead marked by a pole'.

Some *tuns* take their names from rivers, for example Airton 'Aire', Kirk and Castle Leavington 'Leven', Laverton 'Laver', Ryton 'Rye' and Sinnington 'Seven'. The first element of Liverton is probably the name of a stream, meaning 'clotted'.

Place-names signifying the proximity of the *tun* to a topographical feature are numerous: Cropton 'hill-top', Deighton (2), Kirk Deighton and North Deighton 'ditch', Eavestone 'brow of the hill', Garton and Garton on the Wolds 'triangular piece of land', Ingleton 'the hill called *Ing-hyll*', East and West Marton 'pool', Great Mitton and Myton on Swale 'river-confluence', Overton 'bank', Rimington 'boundary' possibly, Rylstone 'brook', Treeton 'trees', Whorlton 'Whorl Hill' (the name of a round hill nearby), Wrelton 'gallows-hill'.

References to the name of the soil or ground are also frequent, as in (West) Clayton 'clay', Flinton 'where flints are found', Grassington 'pasture', Grindleton 'gravelly ground', Hetton 'heath', Horton and Horton in Ribblesdale 'dirty ground', Nether and Upper Poppleton 'pebbly soil', Sancton 'sandy' and Wilton (2) and Bishop Wilton 'wild, uncultivated'. Domestic animals give their names to places such as Calton and Cawton 'calf', Cowton (3) 'cow', Notton 'wether', Oxton 'ox' and Swinton (3) 'pig'. O.E. *bucca* 'buck' is found in Buckton and there is a reference to woodpeckers in Hickleton.

The names of crops occur as first elements in Flaxton, Linton (2) and Linton upon Ouse 'flax', Hayton 'hay', Laughton en le Morthen, East Layton and Leighton 'herb-garden'; and types of vegetation occur in Beeston 'rough grass', in the common Brompton, Brompton upon Swale, Patrick Brompton, Potter Brompton, Brampton Bierlow and Brampton en le Morthen 'broom', Brearton 'briar' and in Green and Kirk Hammerton 'hammer-sedge'. Shipton Y.E. and Shipton Y.N. have a first element O.E. *heope* 'briar'.

The names of woodland trees occur in Allerton Bywater and Chapel Allerton 'alder', Appleton (5) 'apple-tree', Eshton 'ash', Heslington and East and West Heslerton 'hazel', Mappleton 'maple', Kirby Misperton 'medlar', Plompton 'plum-tree', and Salton, Weeton, Little Weighton and Widdington 'willow'. In the common place-name Thornton, often found with an affix, the meaning of *tun* is 'enclosure', the name meaning 'enclosure fenced by thorn-trees'.

Place-names in *tun* with reference to occupations are found in Bickerton 'bee-keeper farm', Great and Little Smeaton Y.N. and Kirk and Little Smeaton Y.W. 'the smith's farm' and Hopperton 'the cooper's farm'. Groups of individuals are referred to in Knapton (2) 'servants' and Wyton 'women'. The first element of Settrington is obscure, but may mean 'robber' or 'ditch'. O.E. *spraec* 'speech' is found in Speeton and the reference is probably to a place where the hundred or assembly met.

A most important group of place-names in *tun* are those compounded with a personal-name, and these are so numerous that for convenience they are listed at the end of the chapter. Many problems arise in connection with the use of personal-names as place-name elements. Doubts may arise as to their genuineness, especially if they are postulated, or interchangeable with topographical terms (for example Ravenfield from O.E. *hraefn*, meaning either 'raven' or a nickname 'Raven'). Their precise historical significance, too, may be uncertain; in a place-name like 'X's *tun*', 'X' might refer to its founder or owner, or to a person who had been given a grant of land or certain rights. Although it has generally been assumed that a personal-name in a place-name that originated early refers to the founder or at least a leader of the community, there is some evidence to suggest that grants of land even at that early stage were more prevalent than was thought hitherto.

Various compound words were formed with *tun* and some of these are commonly found in place-names. O.E. *bere-tun* 'barley-farm' but also used in the general sense of 'corn-farm' and later as 'outlying grange of an estate' occurs as Barton *frequently*, Barton le Street and Barton le Willows. Although not recorded, O.E. **bothl-tun*, meaning 'an enclosure with buildings' is the origin of the very common place-name Bolton, which often occurs with an affix, as in Bolton Abbey, Bolton-on-Dearne and Bolton upon Swale. Another compound word, *deor-tun* 'deer-park', is found in Darton, while **tun-stall*, simply meaning 'farmstead', is the origin of the common Tunstall, and is also found as the second element of Heptonstall 'farmstead where rose-hips grow'.

Another common element is *ham*, meaning 'homestead' but usually 'village'. It is found mainly in the south-east of England and East Anglia, which suggests an early period of use. In Yorkshire it is found mainly in the East Riding and is invariably the final element of a compound place-name. Sometimes the first element is a descriptive adjective as in

20

Clapham 'noisy', relating to a stream, Metham 'poor' and Newholm 'new'. The location of the *ham* is given in Coverham 'on the River Cover', Rotherham 'on the River Rother', Brigham 'near the bridge', Fosham 'on the ditch', Hollym 'near the hollow' and Kirkby Fleetham 'by the stream'. Meltham may mean 'a *ham* where smelting is done', while the first element of Waxholme may be *weax*, the place-name meaning 'a *ham* where bees are kept'. In Bentham, Bramham and Farnham the first elements mean 'bent grass', 'broom' and 'fern' respectively. Harpham is unusual, possibly meaning 'the harper's homestead'. Some place-names are compounded with personal-names, like Bilham 'Billa', Hubberholme 'Hunberg' (feminine), Levisham 'Leofgeat' and Masham 'Maessa'.

O.E. *wic*, a loan word from Latin (*vicus*), originally meant 'a dwelling' but came to have the meaning of 'a farm', especially 'a dairy-farm'. It is a common element in most areas of Yorkshire, although not found so frequently in the North Riding except in the neighbourhood of Ripon. As a simplex name it is found as Wike or Wyke (2), and occasionally as a first element, as in Wighill, Wykeham and Market Weighton. As a final element it is found as -*wick* (-*wich* in some counties), as in Westwick, Bridge and Copt Hewick 'high', Neswick 'on the headland', Welwick 'near the spring' and Withernwick '*wic* belonging to *Withthorn*', a lost village. References to products are contained in Butterwick (2) 'butter', and East Keswick and Dunkeswick 'cheese'. In Kildwick, with O.E. *cild*, we have 'the young man's farm' and in Huntwick the first element means 'hunter'. Cranswick possibly means 'farm frequented by cranes'. As with other common English elements, many place-names with *wic* are compounded with personal-names, a list of such names being given at the end of the chapter.

Several words are compounded with *wic*, the most important compound being *bere-wic*, literally 'barley-farm', but more usually found in the sense of 'an outlying farm belonging to an estate', as in Barwick in Elmet and Ingleby Barwick. In East and West Hardwick the compound *heorde-wic* 'herd-farm' occurs, and in Wistow *wic-stow* 'dwelling-place'.

In many places the conditions of settlement were such that homesteads and villages had to be fortified, and they were indeed sometimes built on the site of an old fortification. Thus *burh*, *ceaster* and *weorc* are found as elements in place-names. The most common is *burh*, meaning 'fortified place' originally, but 'manor' in later names. Its development in place-names shows some diversity, depending on the case-ending of the element. *Bur-*, *Bour-* are found initially and *brough*, *burgh*, *borough* in simplex names or as a final element. Developments from the dative *byrig* are *bury* in simplex form and -*bury* or -*berry* as a final element.

Brough (2) is found in simplex form, and as a first element *burh* occurs in Burley (2), Burghwallis (Wallis was the name of a family holding the manor), Burrill (with O.E. *hyll* 'hill') and Boroughbridge. The element is compounded with an adjective in Aldborough, Aldbrough (2) 'old' and Newburgh 'new'. Horbury 'fortification on muddy land' and Stanbury 'fortification on stony ground' are formed from the dative case. In Ingle-

21

borough the element is compounded with *Ing-hyll* or *Ingel*, meaning 'hill'. Some compounds with personal-names, which are frequently found, are given at the end of the chapter.

A common compound is *burh-tun*, meaning 'fortified enclosure', as found in such place-names as North Burton, West Burton and Kirkburton. It is particularly common with an affix, as in Burton Constable, Burton on Ure, Constable Burton, Cherry Burton, etcetera. The compound *burh-stall*, perhaps meaning 'the site of the fort' occurs in Birstall and Burstall. Another word meaning 'fortification' is *weorc*, found rarely in Yorkshire, but occurring in Aldwark, with O.E. *ald* 'old'.

Latin *castra*, borrowed into Germanic, and developing into Anglian *caester*, meant 'old fortification' and was especially used with reference to forts of Roman origin. Although occurring commonly in the country generally, it is infrequent in Yorkshire, but it is found in Acaster Malbis and Acaster Selby, where it is combined with *a*, an O.Nb. form of O.E. *ea* 'river'. It is also found in Doncaster 'fortification on the River Don' and Tadcaster 'Tata's fortification'; the former was the Roman station of *Danum* and the latter is probably to be identified with *Calcaria*.

There are several words meaning 'dwelling'. Most commonly found is *cot*, meaning 'a cottage' or 'a shed for domestic animals'. In simplex form the nominative plural gives Coates, and the dative plural Cottam. As a first element it is found in Cotness 'headland where there are cottages' and in Cotcliffe 'cliff by the cottage'. O.E. *bothl* 'dwelling' occurs in North and South Newbald. O.E. *croft*, used to denote an enclosure that included a dwelling, frequently survives in simplex form as Croft, as a first element as in Crofton, and as a second element combined with a significant word as in Havercroft '*croft* where oats are grown'. Molescroft contains the personal-name 'Mul'. North Bierley is derived from an unrecorded word **byrel*, also meaning 'cottage'. O.E. *hall* is found in Newall and is frequent in many place-names as *-hall* and Hall. O.E. *(ge)set*, means 'a dwelling', but is also used to mean 'a stable, a fold', and is the second element of Ossett 'fold where thrushes abound', Lissett 'fold in a meadow', Wintersett 'fold used in winter' and Woodsetts 'folds in the wood'. Settle is from *setl* 'dwelling', in simplex form, while Kirkstall 'place where a church stands' has *stall* 'place' as the second element. O.E. *stow*, also meaning 'place', is found in Westow 'place belonging to women'; and Winestead, from *stede* 'place' has the same meaning. Oldstead, also from *stede*, requires no explanation.

The prevalence of woodland and the preoccupation of the Anglian farmers with the work of clearance is shown by the many place-names that incorporate words for 'woods' and 'clearings'. O.E. *leah*, with the original meaning of 'wood' and then 'a clearing in a wood' or 'forest-glade', was a very frequent element in place-names in woodland areas from the early English period until after the Norman Conquest. It is particularly common in the West Riding where there are thick clusters of place-names containing *leah* up the Skell, Nidd, Wharfe, Aire and Calder, and in an area lying to the north of the Don. As might be expected there are also many place-names with an element meaning 'wood' in these areas.

O.E. *leah* was used as a final element with a variety of significant words. A descriptive adjective is found in Bradleys Both 'broad', Healaugh and Healey 'high', Stanley and Stanningley (2) 'stony', and Whitley, Lower and Upper Whitley 'bright'. Location of the clearing is denoted in Burley 'near a fortification', Copley 'on a hill-top' and Leathley 'on the slopes'. Staveley means 'a forest-glade where staves are obtained'. Associations with trees or vegetation are frequent: Apperley Bridge 'apple-tree', Lindley (Otley) 'lime-tree', Sawley (2) 'willow'; and Bentley 'bent grass', Bramley 'broom', Brierley 'briars', Farnley and Farnley Tyas 'ferns', Farsley possibly 'furze', Lelley 'brushwood' and Sproatley 'shoots'.

There is a reference to wild creatures in Bewerley 'beavers', South Hiendley 'hinds', Honley possibly 'woodcock', Ulley 'owls' and Woolley 'wolves'; and to insects in Midgley 'midges'. The first element of Darley is O.E. *deor*, which meant 'animal' as well as 'deer'. The names of crops grown in clearings occur in Barlow 'barley', Lindley (Huddersfield) 'flax', Wheatley 'wheat' and Wortley (Ecclesfield) 'vegetables'; and the names of domestic animals using the clearings are found in Calverley 'calves', Shepley and Shipley 'sheep' and Studley 'stud of horses'. Stokesley may have O.E. *stocc* 'farm' as a first element. There are also many place-names in *leah* compounded with a personal-name and some of these are listed at the end of the chapter.

There are also a few other words meaning 'clearing', one of which, O.E. **rod*, is very common in the West Riding. Many of the place-names containing **rod* were late formations and followed the extensive clearances of woodland made in the Middle Ages. The usual development of **rod* is *royd* and this is very common in simplex form as (The) Royd(s). An example of the element used finally is Mytholmroyd 'clearing where the streams join'. Ryther, also meaning 'clearing', is probably from a derivative, **ryther*. O.E. *stoccing* and *stubbing*, with the same meaning, are frequently found, especially in minor names, as Stocking (3) and Stubbing(s) (4). References to the tree-stumps remaining after the trees had been felled during the clearance of woodland are made in Cridling Stubbs (the affix is from a personal-name '*Cridela'), Hamphall Stubbs (Hamphall is a form of Hampole) and Walden Stubbs (the affix is a personal-name 'Walding'); and clearing by burning is referred to in the place-name Burn from O.E. *bryne*.

Since woodland was so extensive, the Anglo-Saxons had not only a name for forest-glades and clearings, but also for the country that was devoid of woodland. The word used in this specialised sense was *feld*, Mod.E. *field*. This word, normally found as a second element in the sense of 'an open stretch of country' (compare this with the cognate Afrikaans *veld*), is widespread in Yorkshire and is combined with several types of significant words. It is used with a descriptive first element in Aldfield 'old', Bradfield 'broad', Driffield 'stubble' or perhaps 'manured', Leconfield 'with a muddy ditch', Micklefield 'great' and Mirfield 'pleasant'. Use is signified in Austerfield 'sheep-fold' and Threshfield 'threshing'.

23

Birds are referred to in North and South Duffield 'doves', Ravenfield 'ravens' and Warmfield 'wrens', and animals in Darfield 'deer'. Sheffield is '*feld* near the River Sheaf' and Suffield has a first element 'south'. Personal-names denoting ownership or association are found in Huddersfield '*Hudred', Manfield 'Manna' and perhaps in West Tanfield '*Tana'. The meaning of Wakefield is 'a place where a wake is held', no doubt a reference to the Towneley mystery plays presented there.

Mod.E. *land* is derived from O.E. *land*, which was not only used in a general sense but also more specifically in the sense of 'a tract of land' or 'a district'. In this last sense, as a rare first element, it is found in Landmoth 'the district meeting-place'. It occurs as a simplex name in Lands, and as a final element compounded with a descriptive word in Greetland 'gravelly', Newland 'new', Soyland 'marshy' and Cleveland 'hilly district'. Location is described in Norland 'north' and ownership is denoted in Old Byland and Byland Abbey 'Bega's land'.

Another common element, relating to land, especially in the West Riding, is *halh*, usually meaning "a nook' or 'a corner of land', although the actual meaning depends on its use in a particular place-name. Initially it develops usually as *Hal-* or *Haugh-*, and finally as *-hall*, *-all*, *-halgh* or *-ough*. In simplex form its occurs in minor names as Hales or Haugh, and as a first element is often found with *tun* as in Halton. Halton Gill, East and West Halton, Great and Little Houghton. In Halifax it is combined with *feax* to mean 'nook of land where coarse grass abounds'. In compound words it is often used to describe the nature of the ground as in Kirk Sandall and Sandal Magna 'sandy' and Gowdall 'where marigolds grow'. Pannal has O.E. *panne* 'pan' as a first element and probably refers to some nearby hollow. Location is denoted in Skellow 'near the Skell', Wighill 'near the dairy-farm' and Beal 'near the river-bend', while there is possibly a reference to wild cats in Cattal and to snipe in Snydale. North and South Elmsall mean 'a piece of land where elms grow'. Examples of compounds with personal-names, which are frequent, are given at the end of the chapter.

O.E. *hoh*, meaning chiefly 'a spur of land', but with several other meanings, has also a wide and frequent distribution. As a first element with *tun*, it is commonly found as Hutton, most place-names of this type having an affix to distinguish them from other places of the same name, and also as Hooton and as (Glass) Houghton, It is sometimes found in combination with *land* as in Nether and High Hoyland and Hoyland Swain. As a final element it occurs in Sharow 'boundary hill', in Binsoe 'Binte's spur of land' and in Potto, with M.E. *potte* 'hollow'.

The word *aecer*, Mod.E. *acre*, meaning 'a plot of cultivated ground', is combined with **beos* 'bent grass' in Bessacarr, while *balca* 'a ridge' or 'a bank' is found in Balk. O.E. **ric* has a variety of meanings. In Cookridge, where it has been replaced by *hrycg* 'a ridge', the original meaning was probably 'Cwica's strip of land'; in Lindrick, with *lind* 'lime-tree', it may mean either 'strip of land' or 'ditch'. The second element of Wheldrake is most probably **ric*, but its precise significance is not clear; the first element may be O.E. *cweld* 'death' (compare this with Morpeth 'mur-der-path'). Another word meaning 'a narrow strip of land' is O.E. *thwang*, from which Netherthong and Upperthong are derived.

As we have seen, the Angles used many words descriptive of land in forming place-names. There is yet another class of words, referring to the enclosures they made after the ground was cleared. Fences, no doubt often temporary ones in the form of wattle hurdles, and hedges were used for this purpose. O.E. *(ge)haeg*, originally meaning 'fence' and then 'ground enclosed by a fence', especially 'ground fenced off for hunting', is commonly found. As a first element it occurs with *sceaga* 'wood' in Heyshaw, and as a second element with *hnaepp* in Nappa Y.W. and Nappa Hall Y.N., which mean 'enclosure shaped like a bowl'. With a personal-name as a first element it is found in Broxa 'Broc', Embsay 'Embe' and Pudsey 'Pudoc'. A word of similar meaning is *haga*. This frequently occurs as a simplex name as Haigh or Haughs. In Haworth it is combined with *worth*, also meaning 'enclosure', and is therefore prob-ably used here in the sense of 'hedge'. Galphay, an attractive village that belies its macabre name, means 'gallows enclosure'. Stotfold is derived from *stod-fald*, a compound word meaning 'horse enclosure'.

O.E. *worth* is a common element in south Yorkshire in the Doncaster-Sheffield-Barnsley area, in the Bingley-Keighley area and in upper Calder-dale, but is rare in east and north Yorkshire. It occurs once in the North Riding, in Heworth, in combination with *heah* 'high', probably with the meaning of 'principal enclosure'. There is perhaps a reference to the shape of the enclosure in Saddleworth, from *sadol* 'saddle'. In Ingbirchworth 'birch enclosure by a meadow', Roughbirchworth, with *ruh* 'rough', and Oakworth 'oak' we have references to trees, and in Rishworth we have the meaning 'overgrown with rushes'. Most of the place-names with *worth* found in Yorkshire are formed with personal-names and a selection is given at the end of the chapter.

In their advance into north Yorkshire the Angles no doubt used the Roman road they called Leeming Lane, between Boroughbridge and Catterick, and called Watling Street, both north and south of this section, a road that roughly follows the route of the A1. The derivation of Leeming is given in Chapter 2. Watling Street was a name applied to several Roman roads in the country, although originally referring to the road between London and St. Albans, and was derived from *Waeclingastraet*, an early name for St. Albans. In forming place-names the Angles originally used the word *straet*, Mod.E. *street*, in the specialised sense of 'a Roman road', although it later meant 'a paved way' and ultimately 'street'. When used as an element of or an affix with Yorkshire place-names, it is an indication that a Roman road runs nearby. In simplex form it occurs as Street (3), and as a first element with *ford* in Startforth and Lower and Upper Strafforth, and with *tun* in Stirton and Sturton Grange. It is also found as an affix in Adwick le Street, Appleton le Street, Barton le Street, Thornton le Street and Wharram le Street.

The Angles had little interest in communications and references to roads in place-names are few. O.E. *paeth* 'path' is found in Pateley Bridge, while *weg*, Mod.E. *way*, and *hraca* 'narrow path' are found in some minor names. O.E. *geat* 'gate' (compare this with O.N. *gata* 'road') is found in Burnt Yates, although the significance of the place-name is not clear, and *haecc* may have been used in the sense of 'a gate across the road' in Great and Little Heck. The use of *brycg* 'bridge' as a final element is common. Examples are Bainbridge, where it is used in conjunction with a river-name, Stocksbridge, meaning 'bridge made of logs', and Oughti-bridge, where the first element is a woman's name, 'Uhtgifu'.

Since there were few bridges, a place where a river could be forded was important, and so the word *ford* is found frequently. Sometimes, if a bridge was erected later, *brycg* replaced *ford*, or as in Stamford Bridge, meaning 'ford paved with stone', *ford* was retained after the bridge was built. The word is used with a descriptive first element in Barforth in the sense of 'ford used to carry corn', Dishforth 'ditch', Gate and Water Fulford 'dirty', Hackforth, with O.E. *haecc*, possibly in the sense of 'a sluice', Rufforth 'rough' and Yafforth 'river', a reference to the Wiske. Horsforth means 'a ford suitable for horses to cross' and Woodles-ford 'a ford near a thicket'.

First elements referring to topographical features are found in Ample-forth 'where sorrel grows', Brafferton (*tun* has been added to give the meaning 'farm by the broad ford'), South Milford 'by the mill and Spofforth 'by the plot of land'. Salterforth 'ford used by salt-dealers' is no doubt a reference to a salt-way. In Luddenden Foot, which means 'valley where a loud stream flows', the affix was originally *ford*, which as a result of folk etymology was replaced by Foot, a reference to the position of the village at the foot of a hill.

Names of the *-ingas* type, meaning 'the people of', are:—

-ingas:

Fitling 'Fitela', Fylingdales '*Fygela', Gembling '*Gemela', Gilling (2) '*Getla', Kiplin '*Cippela', Leavening '*Lethen', East and West Lilling 'Lilla', Pickering 'Picer'.

-ingaham:

Barningham 'Beorna', Brantingham 'Brant', Collingham 'Cola', Cottingham 'Cotta', North and South Frodingham 'Froda', Goodman-ham 'Godmund', Hovingham '*Hofa', Keyingham '*Caega', Lastingham '*Last', Ottringham 'Oter', Walkingham Hill '*Walca', Wintringham 'Wintra', Yedingham 'Eada'.

-inga- and suffix:

(a) First element a personal-name: Bingley 'Bynna', Finghall '*Fin', Givendale Y.W. 'Gythla', Headingley 'Head(d)a', Killinghall '*Cylla', Knedlington '*Cneoddel', Knottingley '*Cnotta', Whashton 'Hwassa', possibly Sicklinghall '*Sicela'.

(b) First element a folk-name: Billingley 'Billingas', Eastrington 'dwellers living to the east', Spaldington 'Spaldingas', possibly Sleningford 'Sleaningas'.

The first element of Markingfield and Markington may mean 'boundary dwellers' or 'the Mercians'.

In the following place-names 'farmsteads associated with' is to be related to the personal-name shown:—

ing (connective) and *tun:*

Arthington '*Earda', Bainton 'Bega', Boynton 'Bofa', Bridlington 'Berhtel', Darrington 'Deornoth', Dinnington and Dunnington (York) 'Dun(n)a', Dunnington (Skipsea) 'Dud(d)a', Easington (3) 'Esa', Edlington '*Eadel', Ellington 'Ella', Elvington 'Aelfwine', Fawdington '*Falda', Hartlington '*Heortla', Hemlington 'Hemela', Kellington 'Ceolla', North and South Kilvington '*Cylfa', Kirklington '*Cyrtla', Lartington '*Lyrta', Laxton '*Lax(a)', Leppington 'Leppa', Lockington and Lockton '*Loca', Lotherton '*Hluttor', Menston '*Mensa', Millington 'Midele' or 'Mil(l)a', Nunnington 'Nunna', North and South Otterington '*Otor', Ovington 'Wulfa', Parlington '*Pertel', Pocklington '*Pocela', Portington possibly '*Porta', Rainton '*Raegen', Rillington 'Redel', Stillington '*Styfela', Terrington '*Teofor', Waddington 'Wad(d)a', Walkington '*Walca', Waplington possibly 'Waeppela'.

In the following place-names the personal-name is to be associated with the feature denoted by the suffix:—

ing (connective) and suffix:

burh Benningbrough 'Benna', *dun* Huntington 'Hunta', *fleot* Stillingfleet '*Styfela', *ham* Addingham 'Ad(d)a', Manningham 'Maegen', *ofer* Hunsingore 'Hunsige', *wald* Easingwold 'Esa', *worth* Illingworth 'Illa'.

Examples of Old English personal-names with various elements are:—

burh:

Bilbrough 'Bil(l)a', Eggborough 'Ecga', Goldsborough 'Godel', Knaresborough 'Cenheard', Mexborough '*Meoc', Middlesbrough 'Midele', Sprotbrough '*Sprotta', Worsborough 'Wyrca'.

ford:

Aberford 'Eadburg' (feminine), Brinsworth (originally -*ford*) 'Bryni', Lower and Upper Dunsforth 'Dun(n)', Wansford '*Wandel'.

halh:

Bedale 'Beda', Birdsall 'Bridd', Bossall 'Bot', Brignall 'Bryning', Burnsall 'Bryni', Gomersal '*Guthmer', Pickhill '*Pica', Riccall 'Rica', Strensall '*Streon', High and Low Worsall 'Wyrca'.

27

leah:

Alwoodley 'Aethelwald', Ardsley 'Eanred', Armley '*Earma', Auckley '*Alha', Austonley 'Aelfstan', Barnsley 'Beorn', Batley 'Bata', Beamsley 'Bedhelm', Bordley 'Brorda', Cantley '*Canta', Kirk and West Ella 'Aelf(a)', Emley '*Em(m)a', Grantley '*Grante', Guiseley '*Gislic', Helmsley 'Helm', Gate and Upper Helmsley 'Hemele', Hildenley '*Hilding', Keighley '*Cyhha', Otley '*Otta', Pockley '*Poc(c)a', Rodley 'Hrothwulf', Tankersley 'Thancred', Warley 'Werlaf', Weardley 'Wigferth', Hutton Wandesley and Wensley '*Wandel', Whixley '*Cwic', Winksley 'Winuc', Womersley 'Wilmer', Wortley (Armley) 'Wyrca', Yearsley '*Eofor'.

tun:

Adwalton 'Aethelwald', Allerston 'Aelfhere', Barmston 'Beorn', Bilton (3) 'Bil(l)a', Catton and High and Low Catton '*Catta', Cayton '*Caega', Colton 'Cola', Cotherstone 'Cuthere', Ebberston 'Eadbeorht', Great Edstone 'Eaden', Egglestone Abbey '*Ecgel', Egton 'Ecga', Fulstone 'Fugol', Great and Little Habton '*Hab(b)a', Harton possibly '*Herra', Huddleston '*Hudel', Hunton 'Huna', Ilton '*Ylca', Knayton 'Cengifu' (feminine), Lebberston 'Leodbeorht', East and West Lutton 'Luda', Northallerton 'Aelfhere', Picton '*Pica', Sharlston '*Scearf', Silkstone 'Sigelac', Theakston '*Theofoc', Tickton 'Tica', Tollerton '*Tollere', Winton 'Wina', Wombleton 'Wineb(e)ald'.

wic:

Adwick le Street and Adwick upon Dearne 'Adda', Atwick 'Atta', Barnoldswick (2) 'Beornwulf', Bonwick possibly 'Buna', Catwick '*Catta', Earswick 'Aethelric', Elstronwick 'Alfstan', Giggleswick '*Gicel', Heckmondwike 'Heahmund', Kilnwick and Kilnwick Percy '*Cylla', Osbaldwick 'Osbald', Todwick 'Tata'.

worth:

Ackworth 'Acca', Badsworth '*Baeddi', Cartworth '*Craeta', Cudworth 'Cutha', Dodworth 'Dod(d)', Handsworth '*Handwulf', Hawksworth 'Hafoc', Hemsworth 'Hymel(a)', Hepworth '*Heppa', Hunsworth '*Hund', Wadsworth '*Waeddi', Wadworth 'Wad(d)a', Warmsworth '*Wermi', Wentworth 'Wintra', Wigglesworth 'Wincel'.

4. More English Settlement Place-Names

IN the last chapter we saw how the English used a variety of words as elements of habitation-names. Nearly as important were nature-names: hills and valleys, moors, marshes, woods, rivers and streams, lakes and ponds, and the sea were all described; and a multitude of words was used for the purpose.

O.E. *beorg* 'a hill' had a wide distribution, although its modern development is likely to be confused with that of *bearu* 'grove' and *burh* 'fortification', and in Yorkshire with O.N. *berg*, a cognate word also meaning 'hill'. In simplex form it occurs in Barugh, and as a final element in Caldbergh 'cold, bleak', Thornbrough (2) 'thorn', Thrybergh 'three hills' and Welbury 'spring hill'. Another word of wide distribution, found frequently in parts of the West Riding, is *dun*, Mod.E. *down* 'hill'. As a final element it developed as *-don, -den* or even *-ton*, and so is sometimes difficult to distinguish from *denu* or *tun*. In simplex form it is found in Downholme, and in compound form in Cowden 'charcoal', Hedon 'uncultivated' and Yeadon (with *heah* 'high', *h* developing as *y*). In the common place-name Hambleton (all from *dun* except Hambleton (Selby) from *tun*) the first element is O.E. **hamol* in the sense of 'scarred, mutilated', a reference to the shape of the hill.

O.E. *hyll* is commonly found, usually as a final element, although it occurs as a simplex name Hillam, from the dative plural, and as a first element in Hilton. Farnhill, Ryehill (2) and Thornhill are self-explanatory. Tickhill means 'Tica's hill', Toothill 'look-out hill' and Warthill 'beacon hill'.

O.E. *clif* 'a cliff, a steep slope', common in Yorkshire, occurs as Cliffe, and as a first element in Clifford and Clifton. As a final element it is mainly combined with descriptive words as in Arncliffe (2) and Yarncliffe 'eagle', Catcliffe 'bank frequented by wild-cats', Langcliffe 'long', Topcliffe 'top of the cliff', Swarcliffe 'black' and Wycliffe 'white'. Langsett 'long hillside' is derived from *side*, and Stockeld 'tree-stump slope' from *stocc* and *helde*.

O.E. *scelf*, Mod.E. *shelf*, meaning 'a rock, a ledge' or more commonly 'shelving terrain', occurs in Shelf; as a first element in Shelley, with *leah*; and as a final element with personal-names in Hunshelf 'Hun' and Tanshelf '*Taedden'. In the unusual name Bashall Eaves we have *baec*, *scelf* and *efes* with the meaning 'the slope of the ridge at the edge of the wood'.

29

Hartshead 'stag's hill' is derived from *heafod* 'head', used in place-names in the sense of 'a hill, a headland'; and *naess*, also meaning 'a headland', occurs in Reedness 'abounding in reeds' and with a personal-name 'Hacca' in Hackness. Cam Fell is from *camb* 'a crest, a ridge'. References to the shapes of hills are found in Baugh Fell 'rounded', Kirby Knowle 'round-topped' and Wrose 'broken' or 'twisted'. A word meaning 'hill' but more especially 'mound' or 'barrow' is *hlaw*, which develops as a final element as *-low*, *-law* or *-ley*, as in Harlow (2) 'grey' and Rowley 'rough', and with a personal-name in East and West Ardsley 'Eored' and Tinsley '*Tynni'. The word *burgaesn*, also meaning 'a burial place' is found in the common place-name Borrins.

O.E. *stan*, meaning 'stone', commonly occurs as a first element to describe ground, rivers, clearings, etcetera as 'stony'. It was used occasionally as a simplex form as in Stean, and was very common as a second element especially to denote groups of rock or stones in minor names such as Deer Stones, Kidstones, and so on. As a final element it occurs in such place-names as North and South Anston 'the solitary stone', Blaxton 'the black stone', Great and Little Ribston 'stone near which rib-wort grows' and Whiston 'the white stone', no doubt a local feature. Rudston, the first element of which is *rod* 'cross', is named from the huge standing stone to be found in the village churchyard. O.E. *delf* 'quarry' occurs in the unusual place-name Delph.

The word *mor* meant 'moorland' but was also used to mean 'marsh-land'. As a first element it is found with *leah* in Morley and with *tun* in the common Morton and Murton. As a second element it occurs with personal-names in Fadmoor 'Fadda' and Gransmoor 'Grante'. Mod.E. *dale* is largely derived from O.N. *dalr*, cognate with O.E. *dael*, which it usually replaced, although derivation from *dael* is probable where the first element is an Old English word. Examples are: Dalton *frequently*, with *dael* as a first element, 'farm in the valley'; as a second element in Colsterdale 'charcoal-burner', Farndale 'ferns', Grindale 'green', Langstrothdale 'long marsh overgrown with brushwood', Wheel-dale and Wheldale, from O.E. *hweol* 'wheel', a reference to the course of the valley, Wooldale 'wolf', and with a personal-name Bishopdale 'Bis-ceop' and Cundall 'Cunda'. Givendale Y.E. and Y.N. are obscure but are probably derived from river-names. Kirby Grindalythe, consisting of the elements *cran*, *dael* and *hlith*, means 'slopes of crane valley'. The river-name Lune is the first element of Lonsdale.

O.N. *dalr* also replaced O.E. *denu* 'valley' (as in Arkendale with the personal-name 'Eorcon'), although we find *denu* in southern parts of Yorkshire, usually as *Den-* or *-den*. As a first element it is found in Denton, as a second element with a descriptive word in Brogden 'stream', Mixenden 'dung-hill' and Sugden 'swamp'. The first element of Barden Y.W. is *bere* 'barley', while *heope* 'rose-hip' or *heopa* 'bramble' occurs in Hebden and Hebden Bridge. Buckden means 'a valley frequented by bucks' and Ramsden, Shibden and Swinden (3) have references to rams, sheep and swine respectively. River-names are incorporated in Ripponden

'Ryburn' and Skelding 'Skell', and personal-names in Arden '*Earda', Barden Y.N. 'Beorna', Riddlesden 'Rethel', Silsden '*Sigel' and Wilsden 'Wilsige'. Both Todmorden, with (ge)maere, and Marsden, with mercels, mean 'boundary valley', the former also being compounded with a personal-name 'Totta'.

Several place-names are derived from hop, used in the sense of 'a small, secluded valley'. It is found in simplex form in Hope, and as a final element in Bramhope 'broom' and Oxenhope 'oxen'. Eccup means 'Ecca's valley'. O.E. cumb is sometimes found in the sense of 'hollow' as in Horcum 'dirty valley', while in the neighbourhood of Halifax place-names derived from *cloh 'ravine' are common. In simplex form cloh occurs as Clough, which is frequent in minor names, especially with a preceding descriptive adjective. As a first element it occurs in Cloughton. Another common minor name in Yorkshire is Wham(s), from hwamm 'a small valley'.

Several words are used to describe woods or woodland, of which wudu, Mod.E. wood, is the most common. It is found as a first element in Woodhouse and Wothersome, both meaning 'houses in a wood'; and as a second element in such place-names as Cawood 'jackdaw wood', Harewood and Harwood Dale, either 'rocky' or 'hare', Lockwood 'enclosed', Longwood 'long', Meanwood 'a wood owned communally', Norwood 'north' and Whitwood 'white'. East and West Witton, with tun, are derived from widu, an early form of wudu.

An element commonly occurring in Yorkshire, especially south of Leeds and Bradford, with the meaning of 'copse', is sceaga. It is found in simplex form as Shaw (2), and in compound form in Blackshaw 'black', Bradshaw (3) and Brayshaw 'large' and Earnshaw 'eagle'. It is also found with a personal-name in Oughtershaw 'Uhtred'.

Another word with the same meaning, frequent in the West Riding, is hyrst, found as Hirst (4) or Hurst. It also occurs in Hirst Courtney and Temple Hirst. In Holmfirth we have an example of the use of fyrhthe 'wood, woodland', the place-name meaning 'the wood belonging to Holme' (a place nearby, which is derived from holegn 'a holly-tree'), and this is a common element in some areas, especially in minor names. O.E. graf, Mod.E. grove, is the second element of Copgrove 'Coppa's grove' and Howgrove 'grove in the hollow'. Oxspring has spring 'plantation', and Esholt, meaning 'ash wood', has holt, an infrequent element in Yorkshire.

Although the names of trees are commonly used as first elements of place-names, they are not often found in simplex form or as final elements. O.E. thorn, however, is found in Thearne, Thirn and Thorne; as a first element in Thorner 'slope overgrown with thorn-bushes'; and as a second element in Cawthorn and Cawthorne 'cold' and Langthorne 'long'. Birkin is another simplex name, from bircen 'a birch copse'. O.E. treow 'tree' occurs in Bawtry, which has an obscure first element, and in Warter, where it is compounded with wearg 'felon' and means 'gallows'.

The Wolds are derived from wald (compare this with Weald), which means 'high forest land', and the word is found in several place-names,

31

such as Wold Newton, Middleton on the Wolds, and so on. In the period of Anglian settlement the Wolds were more wooded than they are now. In Coxwold 'Cuha's tract of woodland' we have the word as a final element.

There are many place-names consisting of the name of a nearby stream compounded with a descriptive adjective or significant word. O.E. *burna*, meaning 'a spring, stream', is to be found in several place-names, although it is difficult to distinguish from the cognate O.N. word *brunnr*. It occurs as a second element with a word describing its course in Fairburn 'ferns'; and the water itself in Gisburn 'gushing', Great and Little Ouseburn 'flowing into the River Ouse', Saltburn 'salt', possibly from deposits of alum in the locality, Sherburn 'bright' and Colburn 'coal', in other words 'dark'. Slaidburn means 'stream by the sheep pasture', Kirkburn 'stream by the church' and Leyburn 'stream by the clearing', while Welburn (2) also contains *wella* 'spring, stream' as a first element. Kilburn means 'Cylla's stream'. Eastburn, Otterburn and Southburn require no explanation. O.E. *broc*, uncommon in Yorkshire, occurs in Brotton and Broughton 'farmstead by a brook', and also in Darnbrook 'secluded' and Greasebrough 'grassy'.

O.E. *wella* 'a well, spring, stream' occurs in simplex form in Well. In compounds with a descriptive first element we have Caldwell 'cold', Letwell possibly 'with a conduit', and Whitwell and Whitwell on the Hill 'white'; and denoting location, such place-names as Hipswell perhaps 'hill-stream', Rothwell 'by the clearings', Shadwell 'spring in a shady place' and Welton 'farmstead near the spring'. Personal-names are found in Elmswell 'Helm', Harswell '*Hersa', Hauxwell 'Heafoc', Hinderwell 'Hild' (feminine), Hudswell '*Hudel' and Wombwell '*Wamba'. Churwell means 'the peasants' well'.

O.E. *fleot*, meaning 'an estuary' or 'a creek', also had the sense of 'a stretch of river', and this may well have been its meaning where it occurs in Yorkshire place-names, which are mostly the names of villages on the Ouse or Humber. Thus Broomfleet is 'Brungar's stretch of river', while Faxfleet refers to the coarse grass growing there. Ousefleet may signify a creek on the Ouse. The exact significance of Swinefleet is not clear, although the first element may be *swin* 'creek, channel', from which Swine is also derived. In Adlingfleet we have 'the prince's stretch of river', and in Hunslet 'Hun's creek', presumably some inlet of the River Aire. O.E. *foss* 'a ditch', occurs with personal-names in Catfoss 'Catta' and Wilberfoss 'Wilburg' (feminine). O.E. *lacu* 'stream' is found in Elslack 'Aelli's stream' and in Fishlake 'fish-stream'. An old stream name, from *caf* 'swift', is probably to be found in North and South Cave.

O.E. *sae* was used in a variety of senses and could be used to mean anything from 'the ocean' to 'a small lake' or even 'a marsh'. With *mere* 'lake' it is found in Seamer (2) and Semer Water, which may mean 'lake among the marshes'. In Kilnsea we have 'pool near the kiln', in Rotsea 'pool containing refuse', in Seaton and Seaton Ross 'farmstead near a lake', in Woodmansey 'the woodman's pool', and in Burton Pidsea 'pool

32

in the marsh'. Hornsea, containing O.E. *horn* 'horn', may refer to the shape of the lake, and Withernsea, a difficult place-name, may possibly mean 'lake near the thorn-tree'. In Chapel and West Haddlesey the first element *haethel* may perhaps mean 'heathland' or may even be the name of a lake.

Place-names compounded with *mere* 'lake, pool' and descriptive first elements are: Bulmer 'frequented by bulls', Eldmire 'swans', Fimber 'coarse grass', Redmire 'reedy' and Sledmere 'valley'. Hampole has the meaning 'Hana's pool', the second element being derived from *pol* 'pool', while Lumb is derived from **lumb*, which has the same meaning. Other words for 'pond' or 'pool' are M.E. *stank*, from which Stanks is derived, and *wel*, as in Weel, perhaps here 'deep place in a river'.

Long Marston, with *tun*, Marishes and Marske (2) are derived from *mersc* 'marsh', while *fenn*, with the same meaning, gives Fenton (2) 'farmstead in the marsh' and Fenwick 'dairy-farm in the marsh'. Adel, from *adela*, means literally 'a dirty place', no doubt a reference to the marshy nature of the ground, and Kilnsey, from *cyln* and **saege*, means 'marsh near the kiln'.

Elland, meaning 'land by the river', is derived from the compound word *ea-land*, which also meant 'island'. A word with a similar meaning, *eg*, is found in Sessay and Hutton Sessay 'Secg's land by the streams', and in East and West Harlsey, perhaps 'Herel's island'. The unusual place-name Tong is derived from *twang*, *tang*, literally 'tongs', and used in the sense of 'river-fork'. O.E. *staeth*, found in Staithes, meant 'shore' or 'bank of a river' and had a later meaning of 'landing-place'. An element commonly found is *sand* 'sand', as in Sandsend, with *ende* 'end', Sand Hutton, etcetera. O.E. *boga* originally meant 'a bow', but this meaning was extended to 'something curved', and then used to mean 'a river-bend' as in Bowland and Bowes. Another word with the same meaning is *cramb*, as found in Buttercrambe, with *butere* 'butter', which is used in a transferred sense, the place-name meaning 'fertile place where the river bends'. Other words meaning 'river-bend' are *wraesel*, as in Wressell, and **huc*, as in Hook.

The place-names described in this and the previous chapter give some indication of the variety of elements used by the Anglo-Saxons in their formation. The interpretation of most of these place-names is quite straightforward, but for a substantial number this is only tentative, and if space permitted, the question of other possibilities could be explored. Some place-names are even more doubtful. It may be that their derivation is known but the precise significance of the elements used is not understood, or the etymology of the name may be quite obscure. A few of these difficult place-names, for which there is as yet no really satisfactory explanation, are given below.

One example is Baildon, which seems to be derived from O.E. *begel* 'bend' and *dun* 'hill', the latter obviously a reference to the hill on which the place stands. The first element could conceivably be a reference to its circular shape, but another suggestion is O.E. *beg-hyll* 'a hill where berries grow'. Beverley is another difficult name. The first element seems to be *beofor* 'beaver', but the early spellings of the name show *-lic* instead of *-ley* from *leah*, as might be expected. The suggestion has been made that *-lic* is derived from an unrecorded word **licc* 'stream'. In Bardsey, the first element is a personal-name 'Beornred' and the second element is apparently O.E., eg 'island', but this is unlikely in view of the topography of the place, and so the possibility has been put forward that the second element is *(ge)haeg* 'enclosure' or *heah* 'high place'. It has been suggested that Liversedge means 'Leofhere's ridge', but there are objections on topographical grounds and the second element may possibly be 'sedge'. Authorities differ as to the etymology of Filey: it may be a compound of O.E. *fif* and *leah* and so mean 'five clearings'; or it may have O.N. *fifa* 'cotton-grass' as a first element. Paull, near Hull, of uncertain etymology, may mean 'boundary mark'. Eskeleth has *hlith* 'slope' as the second element, but the first is quite obscure. Pool in Wharfedale is not from O.E. *pol* 'pool', but is from **pofel*, also found in Pollington, and of doubtful meaning. Snainton is another obscure name. Spen, as in Spen Valley, Spennithorne, and so on, occurring frequently in Yorkshire, is an element for which there is no satisfactory explanation. Suggestions have included 'enclosure', 'footbridge', 'ditch' and 'lane'. Swillington, another difficult name, may possibly mean 'farmstead near a place called Swine-hill'. The derivation of Timble is doubtful, although it may be from **tymbel*, used in the sense of 'the tumbling stream'. That delightful name, Tocketts, has a second element *cot* 'cottage', but the first element defies explanation. Wawne, another doubtful name, may possibly mean 'marsh-land', while Warsill, the second element of which is uncertain, may mean 'watchman's nook of land' or 'watch-tower'.

5. Methods of Place-Name Formation

IN Chapter 1 the most important methods of place-name formation were described, namely the use of elements singly or compounded together. The Anglo-Saxons also had three other ways in which they fashioned place-names: by the use of case endings, prepositions and adverbs, and affixes.

Words contained in place-names are often found in the singular or plural of the genitive or dative case. The genitive, which is found mostly in compounds, is normally, but not invariably, used to denote ownership. An -*es* genitive singular ending occurs in *Bernulfesuuic* and *Badesuuorde*, the *Domesday Book* forms of Barnoldswick 'Beornwulf's dairy-farm' and Badsworth 'Baeddi's enclosure' respectively, while the northern form of this ending, -*is*, is found in Barkisland 'Bark's tract of land'. In the North place-names occur sometimes without the genitival ending, as in Allerton Mauleverer 'Aelfhere's farmstead'.

Many place-names, especially in Yorkshire, had the sense of '(a place) at the . . .', and were formed by using the preposition 'at' and the definite article before the name itself, which was in the dative case. These later developed as *atten* or *atter*, and then became M.E. *atte*. Thus Attercliffe simply means '(a place) at the cliff'. But in most cases the preposition was lost later and the form simply appeared in the dative case. This explains a place-name such as Reeth, which was originally *aet thaem rithe* 'at the stream'.

Most frequently, however, the form occurred in the dative plural, which ended in -*um*, and many Yorkshire place-names are formed in this way. In the following representative list '(a place) at the' or '(a place) amongst the' is to be understood: Acomb 'oak-trees', Angram (3) 'pastures', Beadlam 'buildings', Byram 'cowsheds', Crambe 'bends (of the river)', Harome 'rocks', Hipperholme 'osiers', Kilham 'kilns', Northowram and Southowram 'slopes', Rise 'brushwood', Stittenham and Yapham 'steep places', Thorneholme 'thorn-trees' and Yarm 'fish-pools'.

The place-name Nosterfield, as well as showing use of the dative, provides an example of metanalysis, or wrong division of words. Thus the early spelling *aet thaem eowestre felde* 'at the sheepfold field' first developed into *atten eostrefelde*, the -*n* of *atten* became attached to *eostrefelde*, which became Nosterfield, and *atte* was then lost. Metanalysis has also probably occurred in the place-name Nostell Priory from *osle* 'blackbird' and *leah* 'clearing'.

Prepositions and adverbs were also used extensively in place-name formation. Their use with the name itself was to help to describe its precise location or to distinguish it from another place of the same name. In Beeford 'by the ford' and Allerton Bywater 'by the water' we have examples of the use of the preposition *bi* 'by' or 'near'. O.E. *fore* 'in front of' occurs in Fordon, meaning 'in front of the hill', and *under* 'below' in Thorpe Underwood. In Upleatham 'at the upper slopes', with *hlith* in the dative plural, *upp* is used to show that the place is higher than Kirkleatham. Upton 'higher farmstead' shows a similar use. In Dunkeswick 'cheese-farm' we have *dune* 'down, lower' and *ofan* in Ovenden, meaning '(land) above the valley'. The preposition *mid* occurs in Middop, which means '(land) between the valleys', while *ut* 'out' is often used in the sense of 'remote' in such place-names as Outwood, Out Newton 'remote new farmstead' and Owthorne 'the remote thorn-tree'. O.E. *sundor* 'apart' was used to mean 'private', as in Sunderlandwick 'dairy-farm on private land'. The use of prepositions in place-names like Kingston upon Hull, Myton on Swale and Burton in Lonsdale needs no explanation. Sometimes Latin *super* 'above, on' and *sub* 'below' were used, as in early spellings of Newton on Ouse and Sutton under Whitestone Cliffe.

Affixes were also used, singly, but more often in pairs, to identify a place more precisely and to distinguish between two or more places of the same name, especially between a secondary settlement and a parent village. Most commonly found are affixes denoting direction, and so we have such place-names as North and South Anston, East and West Hardwick. Sometimes the affix was used to show the location of one place in relation to another, as in Sutton Howgrave and Howgrave, the former lying to the south of the latter. 'Lower' and 'Upper' are found in Lower and Upper Dunsforth, Lower and Upper Strafforth, Lower and Upper Whitley, while other variations are found in Nether and Over Silton, Nether and Upper Poppleton, High and Low Catton, and High and Nether Hoyland. Sometimes *middel* 'middle' was used to describe position by reference to other places, as in Middleton *frequently*, Middleton upon Leven, Middleton Quernhow, etcetera. In Middleham its significance has been lost since the reference to other places is not known. Sometimes a township is designated by the term *Both* as in Bradleys Both and Martons Both.

Pairs of affixes often denote size, as in Great and Little Ayton, Barugh, Heck, etcetera. 'Great' is sometimes denoted by Latin *magna* as in Hutton Magna and 'small' by *parva* as in Ruston Parva. O.E. *micel* 'great' is often combined with another element as in Mickleton and Micklefield, both of which have been influenced by the cognate O.N. *mikill*. As an affix *micel* survives as *Much* (for example Much Wenlock), although Yorkshire has no examples of this type.

Place-names defining a place by reference to a locality are Marton in Cleveland, Foston on the Wolds, Burley in Wharfedale, Thornton in Lonsdale, Thorpe in Balne, and so on. Affixes denoting a situation in woodland are found in such place-names as Bolton by Bowland and Marton in the Forest, and a situation in moorland in such place-names as Barmby on the Moor and Holme upon Spalding Moor. Proximity to a cliff is shown in Sutton under Whitestone Cliffe, while there are references to marshland in Barmby on the Marsh and Full Sutton 'dirty, swampy'.

Place-names denoting a situation on a river, as in Adwick upon Dearne, Clifton on Ure, Dalton upon Tees, and Ellerton on Swale are common. Appleton Wiske, Kirby Wiske, Kirkby Wharfe and Water Fulford are elliptical[1] forms. Position on a road is denoted by such place-names as Appleton le Street and Barton le Street, and Gate Helmsley and Gate Fulford.

The nature of the ground is indicated in a place-name like Norton le Clay, and vegetation and crops are referred to in Newton le Willows and Thornton le Beans. Potter Brompton and Potter Newton were places where pottery was made, Glass Houghton was a place where glass was blown, and Kirkby Overblow, from *or-blawere*, a place where smelting was carried on.

Descriptive affixes are used in Copt Hewick (from *coppede* 'with a peak') and Bridge Hewick to distinguish between them. We have Old Byland and Old Malton, and various places with *niwe* 'new', where the word may be an affix or a first element, as in Newbiggin or the frequent Newton, and use of the adjective 'long' in Long Preston. Cold Kirby and Coniston Cold have *cald* 'cold' in the sense of 'bleak, exposed'; and Hanging Grimston and Hanging Royd have *hangende* 'hanging, steep'. Where two villages have been joined together, sometimes both the old names are used to form a new place-name, as in Hutton Wandesley, Kirkby Fleetham and Thornton Watlass.

Several affixes or elements relating to Christianity were used in place-names after the conversion of the Anglo-Saxons during the seventh century. Although no place-name derived from O.E. *mynster* is to be found in Yorkshire (compare this with Kidderminster, Warminster), Mod.E. *minster* is used with reference to the cathedrals at York and Ripon, which were early centres of Christian settlement and teaching. O.E. *cirice* 'church' is found as an affix in Church Fenton and was probably a common element in place-names, but has been replaced or influenced by O.N. *kirkja*. This occurs as a first element in such place-names as Kirby, South Kirkby, Kirkham, Kirkhamgate and Kirkleatham; as a final element in Oswaldkirk and Whitkirk; and more commonly as an affix, in the form Kirk in Kirk Barmwith, or with an affix, as in Kirby Hill (2), Knowle and Misperton, and in Kirkby Malham, Moorside and Wharfe.

Place-names such as Bishop Monkton, Moor Monkton, Monk Bretton and Monk Fryston show a connection with monasteries and Nun Monkton with a nearby nunnery also. Nunwick means 'the nuns' dairy-farm'

---

[1] Elliptical here means that the prepositions in the names denoting their situation have been omitted.

although nothing is known about any connection with a particular nunnery. Preston, Great Preston, Long Preston, Preston under Scar and Purston Jaglin were places that were probably in the possession of priests. Several places, such as Bishop Burton, Bishop Monkton, Bishop Thornton, Bishop Wilton, were so named because they were in the possession of the Archbishop of York. Acaster Selby was so named because the manor was held by Selby Abbey. The affix *tempel* in Temple Hirst and Temple Newsam indicates an association with the Knights Templars.

Some place-names commemorate the names of saints. Burton Leonard is named after St. Leonard, while Felixkirk, Oswaldkirk and Romaldkirk were places whose churches were dedicated to St. Felix, St. Oswald and St. Romald respectively.

6. The Scandinavian Element

FOR over two centuries the activities of the Vikings—Danes, Norwegians and Swedes—seriously affected, and indeed almost destroyed, the social fabric of Western Europe. England itself was almost overwhelmed by their attacks: at first forces of Vikings descended on coastal areas and penetrated inland in savage raids; then a period of invasion by an army occurred; and ultimately extensive colonisation of the eastern half of the country took place. Such a settlement had a deep influence on the social and economic organisation of the English people, but particularly on their language.

Although Scandinavians and English could understand each other without difficulty, since their languages, developed from North and West Germanic respectively, were ultimately derived from a parent Germanic language, there were many linguistic differences. Furthermore, there were two branches of Scandinavian spoken by the invaders: the Danes spoke East Scandinavian and the Norwegians West Scandinavian. Although English ultimately became the dominant language, an Anglo-Scandinavian dialect was spoken in some parts of the country for over two centuries. English enriched its vocabulary by taking many words from Scandinavian, such borrowings consisting of basic words like *egg*, *root*, *husband*, *sky*, *skin*, *wing*, etcetera, and even the pronouns *they*, *their* and *them*. English grammar and syntax, however, remained largely unaffected. Scandinavian influence on English place-names has also been considerable, especially in those parts of the country where extensive colonisation occurred.

There were two periods of Viking activity affecting England: the period 865-954, during which time an extensive settlement of Scandinavians took place; and a second period of military struggle from about 980 until after the Norman Conquest, during which time the rulers of Denmark attempted to subdue the English kingdom. In the first phase after a series of raids on various parts, a Danish army under the sons of Ragnar Lothbrok, a famous Viking, landed in East Anglia. The Danes divided their forces in 874: one army moved southwards to attack Wessex and afterwards colonised part of Mercia and East Anglia; the other army moved northwards, and in 876 was centred on York, where Halfdan, its commander, distributed much of the land of Yorkshire among its members. By a treaty made in 886, the border was stabilised between that part of England colonised by the Danes, known as the Danelaw, and the rest of England.

From about 900 another invasion, this time by Norwegian Vikings, began on the north-west coast of England, and their settlements took in Cumberland, Westmoreland, Lancashire, Cheshire and the north-western parts of Yorkshire. Previously Norwegians had invaded and colonised parts of Ireland, the Isle of Man and the Scottish islands, and the colonisation that now took place was made by invaders from these places, not from Scandinavia itself. The kingdom of Northumbria was so weak that it was unable to prevent this penetration, which resulted from infiltration rather than military conquest. The close connection which existed between Dublin, the capital of the Viking state in Ireland, and York, where a Viking kingdom had been established, no doubt served to encourage settlement of the north-west. With the fall of the kingdom of York in 954, the Scandinavians of the Danelaw submitted to English rule.

Although the outline of events relating to the Scandinavian invasions is firmly established, little is known about the actual character and extent of the settlement, and many problems arise. In the absence of historical records much depends on the interpretation of place-name evidence, for the distribution and concentration of place-names and their linguistic characteristics offer some guide as to the pattern of settlement.

Since the languages spoken by Danes and Norwegians, East and West Scandinavian respectively, were very similar, many words used as place-name elements were common to them both. There were, however, some words used as elements that were peculiar to one language only. Place-names that incorporate such words as *thorp*, *both*, *hulm* and *toft*, for instance, are likely to be of Danish origin, and their presence in place-names is an indication of Danish, as apart from Norwegian, settlement. Sometimes the actual meaning of a place-name provides such evidence. Such place-names as Danby, Denby, Denaby and Danthorpe, all mean 'village of the Danes' although they would most likely indicate isolated Danish settlements. The nucleus of Danish settlement, which was very intensive in many parts of Yorkshire, was York, for it was at this place that Halfdan distributed land to his soldiers, and the strength of Scandinavian influence in York is still evident by the number of its Scandinavian street-names.

Although colonisation by Danish Vikings arose as a result of military conquest, there is no evidence to show that the settlement was other than peaceful, and Danes and English appear to have lived together side by side in amity. The settlement was concentrated in the lowlands and valleys, in particular the valleys of the Rye and Derwent, Ouse, the lower reaches of the Swale and Ure, and much of the Vale of York. Danby on Ure and Danby Wiske may represent the western limits of this settlement. There was another concentration on the coast near Flamborough, and near Malton on the upper Derwent, along the Humber west of Hull, between the Aire and Ouse west of York and in the lower Don valley.

Test-words providing evidence of Norwegian settlement are *brekka* 'hill', *buth* 'booth', *erg* and *skali* 'shieling', *gil* 'ravine', *slakkr* 'shallow valley', among others. Place-names like Normanby (2) and Normanton,

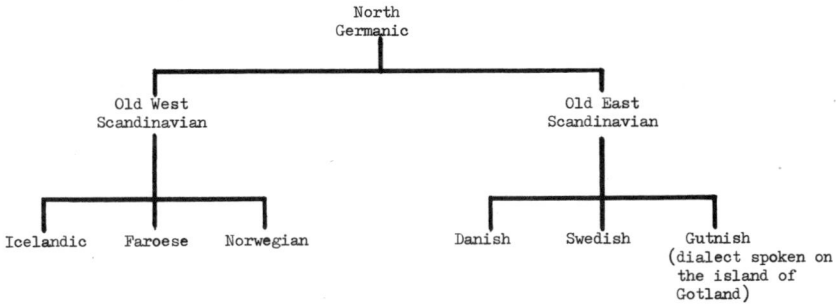

Fig. 4: The North Germanic Languages

meaning 'village of the Northmen', indicate isolated settlements of Norwegians in predominantly Danish areas. Norwegian settlements, perhaps isolated, are also indicated by the following: Irby and Irton, meaning 'village of the Irishmen', referring to Irishmen who came to England with the Norwegians; Scotton (2) 'farm of the Scots or Irish', with a similar meaning; and Birkby Y.N., Monk Bretton and West Bretton, along with Burton Salmon (originally *Bretta-tun*), all meaning 'village of the Britons' and referring to Britons, perhaps from Cumbria, who had accompanied the Norwegian settlers. It is to be noted that Birkby, near Huddersfield, is of different origin and means 'village overgrown with birch-trees'.

Various names incorporating O.Ir. personal-names also occur, and these likewise indicate places where individual Norwegians from Ireland or Irishmen had settled. Examples of such place-names are: Carperby 'Cairpre', Commondale 'Colman', Cononley 'Conan', Duggleby 'Dubhghall', Feizor and Fixby 'Fiach', Gatenby 'Gaithen', Melmerby (Coverdale) 'Maelmuire', Melsonby 'Maelsuithan', Patrick Brompton and possibly Patrington 'Patric', and Yockenthwaite 'Eogan'.

The distribution of place-names of Norwegian origin indicates that these settlements were smaller and less significant than those of the Danes, and were confined to those parts of Yorkshire adjacent to the Lancashire and Westmoreland borders, Teesdale, the upper parts of Swaledale, Wensleydale and Nidderdale, Craven and around Huddersfield. There were other settlements in Cleveland, on the north-east coast near Whitby, and in an area that extended from Ryedale to the northern edge of the Wolds. It is possible that some of these settlements on or near the coast were established by Norwegians coming over the North Sea or by bands of Norwegians from the Viking kingdom of York.

Although many of these settlers, both Norwegian and Danes, must have become familiar with the rivers of Yorkshire in reaching their places of settlement, their names, to some extent Anglian, but largely Celtic in origin, bear little trace of Scandinavian influence. In Wensleydale,

Yorkshire's shortest river, the Bain, takes its name from O.N. *beinn* 'straight', while both the rivers Greta, one an affluent of the Tees and the other an affluent of the Wenning, take their name from O.N. *grjot* 'gravelly, stony'. The river-name Rawthey, derived from O.N. *rauthr* 'red' and *a* 'river', is a reference to crops of red sandstone forming its banks. The Skell is derived from *skjallr* 'resounding' and Skirfare from *skirr* and *far*, meaning 'bright river'. Seph may possibly mean 'slow' and the river-name Hull may be derived from a Danish word *hul*, meaning 'hollow'. The place-name Hull takes its name from the river, although its full name of Kingston upon Hull dates from 1292 when Edward I bought some land there and the place was called 'the king's town'.

Of habitative elements of place-names, easily the most common, and the most widely distributed, is *by*. It has no simplex names, is very rare as a first element, and as a second element is mostly compounded with a Scandinavian personal-name. Since it was used indiscriminately by Danes and Norwegians its use is no pointer to origin, except in one respect; in the north-western parts of Yorkshire, where Norwegian settlement was most evident, it seems to have had the meaning of 'farmstead' or 'hamlet', although elsewhere it usually had the meaning of 'village'. It survived for many years as a place-name element and was a living element after the Norman Conquest as we see by the late name Jolby, which is derived from an O.Fr. personal-name 'Johel'.

There are so many personal-names compounded with *by* that it is more convenient to show a list of them at the end of the chapter. Some are of doubtful origin: Crosby may be derived from O.Ir. *cros* 'a cross' or the O.N. by-name 'Krokr'; Kexby may be from 'Keikr' or from M.E. *kex*, meaning 'dry stalks'; and Killerby may be from O.N. '*Ketilferth' or an O.E. personal-name '*Ceolfrith'.

Compounds with Scandinavian or Old English words are to be found. First elements may denote topographical features as in Barrowby and Borrowby (2) 'hill', Burnby 'stream', Dalby 'valley', Huby (Easingwold) 'spur, ridge' and Wauldby, meaning 'farmstead on the Wolds'. Melmerby (Ripon) means 'farmstead on sandy soil'. The adjectives 'new', in the sense of 'newly-built', and 'large' are found in Newby *frequently* and Mickleby respectively. There are references to people in Hunmanby 'houndsman' and Whenby 'women'. Tree-names are found in Selby 'willow' and Eppleby 'apple'. The first element of Quarmby is O.N. *kvern* 'a mill' or 'a mill-stone'. Fearby, possibly from O.N. *fiother* 'four', may indicate the number of dwellings that formed the hamlet.

As we have seen by such place-names as Denby, Denaby, and so on, *by* is sometimes combined with a word denoting a race of people. Other examples are Ingleby Arncliffe, Ingleby Barwick and Ingleby Greenhow, which refer to settlements of English, probably isolated, in north Yorkshire, and the interesting place-name Ferrensby, which means 'farmstead of a man from the Faroe Islands'. During the period of settlement, no doubt the Danes, like the Norwegians, were accompanied by numbers of people of different origins.

After *by*, the next most common Scandinavian element is *thorp*. This is found over the whole of Yorkshire, with particular concentrations near Sheffield and Wakefield. Since it is found only in Old East Scandinavian, it is a useful test-word indicating settlement by Danes. The cognate O.E. *throp* was also used as a place-name element, but although prevalent in many parts of England, its use is rare in the Danelaw. *Thorp* was used in the sense of 'a secondary settlement' or 'outlying farm' and continued in use in the Middle English period. It commonly occurs as the simplex name Thorpe, although many names of this type have an affix, for example Thorp Arch, Thorpe le Street, Thorpe on the Hill, Thorp Perrow, Thorpe Stapleton, etcetera. Although rare as a first element, it is frequently found as a second element. Sometimes in combination it indicated dependence on or location in relation to another place: an example of the former is Littlethorpe, which was a grange of Ripon; Austhorpe 'east' and Middle-thorpe 'middle' are examples of the latter. Newthorpe is self-explanatory.

As with *by*, compounds of place-names in *thorp* with personal-names are very common and are accordingly listed at the end of the chapter. O.E. 'Earnwulf' or O.Dan. 'Arnwulf' may be the first element of Arm-thorpe, and either O.E. 'Cola' or O.N. 'Koli' the first element of Cow-thorpe. The early form of Claxton was *Claxtorp*, *thorp* being replaced by *tun*; the first element is 'Klak', an O.Dan. personal-name. O.N. *konungr* is the first element of Coneythorpe and Coneysthorpe, which mean 'the king's outlying farmstead', while O.N. *kaup-mathr* 'merchant' is contained in Copmanthorpe. Ellenthorpe incorporates O.E. *aetheling* 'prince' and Nunthorpe has *nunne*, from an order of nuns who resided there.

Another O.N. place-name element, common in north-western Yorkshire although rare in the East Riding, is *thveit*, which has developed as *thwaite*. The word means 'a woodland clearing' and later 'a meadow', and although not distinctively Norwegian, is probably found more in north-western parts, where Norwegians settled, simply because these are the parts where much woodland and waste had to be cleared. It occurs frequently as a simplex name, Thwaite, and also in compounds as a second element. O.N. personal-names are found in Gunthwaite 'Gunnhildr' (feminine), Hampsthwaite 'Hamall' and Hunderthwaite 'Hun(d)ra'. Micklethwaite means 'the great clearing' and Hebblethwaite 'clearing near a plank bridge'. Bouthwaite is 'a clearing with a store-house' and (Carlton) Husthwaite 'a clearing where houses have been erected'. Thornthwaite incorporates a tree-name 'thorn', while Linthwaite contains O.N. *lin* 'flax'. Swinithwaite means 'a place cleared by burning'. Slaithwaite, with its distinctive local pronunciation (slauwit), may be derived from O.E. *slah*, meaning 'a clearing where sloes grow', or from O.N. *slag*, in the sense of 'a clearing where trees are felled'.

The element, *hulm* or *holmr*, in the sense of 'a water-meadow' or 'a piece of dry ground in a marsh' is distributed widely in Yorkshire and occurs particularly frequently in flat, low-lying areas. The element had the form *hulm* in Old Danish, giving *hulme* in place-names, and the form *holmr* in Old West Scandinavian, giving *holme*. It would appear that most forms in Yorkshire are from *holmr*, on the basis of subsequent development, even though they are prevalent in areas of Danish settlement (where one would expect *hulm*), but this may be explained by the fact that during the Middle English period *u* and *o* were often spelt as *o*, and so the elements cannot be distinguished.

The simplex form Holme occurs frequently, while there is an example of the rare use of *holmr* as a first element in Holmpton, which probably means 'farm by the sea-shore'. A descriptive word is used with the element to form place-names such as Denholme 'water-meadow in the valley', Skyreholme 'bright water-meadow' and Sleightholme 'flat water-meadow'. Sometimes a personal-name is found as in Balkholme 'Balki's water-meadow' and Benningholme 'Benna's water-meadow'. O.E. *haenep* occurs in Hempholme, meaning 'hemp field'.

Personal-names incorporating the word *toft* (O.Dan. *toft*, O.N. *topt*) are widely distributed in Yorkshire but commonest in its southern parts. It means 'a curtilage' or 'a messuage'[1] and suggests Danish rather than Norwegian settlement. As a first element it is rare but is frequently found as a simplex name in the form Toft. As a second element it is often compounded with an adjective or descriptive word as in the following: Altofts 'old', Blacktoft 'black', probably a reference to the colour of the ground, Eastoft 'ash-wood', Hartoft 'stony', Langtoft 'long', Thrintoft 'thorn-bush' and Willitoft 'willow'. The unusual place-name Burman-tofts incorporates M.E. *burh-man* and means 'messuages belonging to the townsman'.

Many place-names have been formed from Scandinavian words denoting natural features. From O.N. *berg* 'hill', cognate with O.E. *beorg*, we have Aikber 'oak-tree hill'. Sedbergh is derived from *set-berg* 'a flat-topped hill'. O.N. *haugr*, meaning 'a hill' but also 'a tumulus, a mound', occurs in the simplex form Howe, and is an element of Cracoe 'crow hill', Gledhow 'kite hill' and Meugher, with O.N. *mjor*, 'small hill'. In Sexhow *haugr* is combined with a Scandinavian personal-name and means 'Sek's mound', while in Claro we have a similar form with an O.E. personal-name 'Clare'. Stanghow, with O.N. *stong* in the sense 'marked by a pole', Ainderby Quernhow, with O.N. *kvern* 'mill-stone', and Ingleby Greenhow, with O.E. *grene* 'green', also have *haugr* as a second element. There are many place-names like Shunner Howe (with an O.N. personal-name 'Sjonr' as a first element), which have *haugr* as an affix.

O.N. *fjall* is found as *fell*, as in Cracoe Fell, Fountains Fell, and the like. O.N. *hryggr*, cognate with O.E. *hrycg*, which gives Mod.E. *ridge*, often develops as *rigg* in many Yorkshire minor names, but is found as *-rick* in Marrick, meaning 'a ridge where horses are kept'. Cowlam, meaning 'at the hill-tops', is from the dative plural of O.N. *kollr*, and Clint is derived from O.Dan. *klint*, meaning 'rocky cliff'. Gragareth, a long ridge situated near Whernside, is derived from O.N. *grar* and *grjot*

---

[1] Curtilage is an area attached to a dwelling house. Messuage is a dwelling house with outbuildings and land assigned to its use.

and means 'grey stones'. Hawes is from O.N. *hals*, meaning 'a pass', and this is also the first element of Halsham, although its precise meaning is uncertain here.. Acklam (2) and Hallam are dative plurals, both meaning 'slopes'. O.N. *hlith* 'slope' is found in Lythe, and is combined with an O.N. personal-name in Hanlith. The place-name element *scar*, found frequently in the Dales, is from O.N. *sker*, while O.N. *skarth* occurs in Aysgarth, which means 'pass where oak-trees grow'.

O.N. *dalr* 'valley' is a common element but difficult to distinguish from the cognate O.E. word *dael*, with the same meaning. Place-names incorporating *dalr*, all with O.N. personal-names are: Apedale 'Api', Bilsdale 'Bildr', Bransdale 'Brandr', Garsdale 'Garthr', Raisdale '*Royth(i)r', Rosedale 'Russi', Thixendale 'Sigsten'. O.N. *botn*, meaning 'valley bottom', is found in Starbotton. The first element is derived from O.N. *stafir* 'stake' and so means 'a valley where stakes are found'. The place-name Slack, from O.N. *slakki*, found in areas of Norwegian settlement, means 'shallow valley'. Place-names containing two other O.W.Scand. words, both meaning 'ravine', are also found: Gayle or Gayles from *geil* and such names as Ramsgill from *gil*. Words meaning 'a hollow' are: *gryfja*, found in Falsgrave, with an O.N. personal-name 'Hvalr', and Mulgrave 'Muli'; *hol*, as in Holbeck, with O.N. *bekkr* 'stream', and Holwick, with O.N. *vik*, meaning 'ravine in the hollow'; and possibly *malh*, with the meaning of 'baglike hollow', as in Malham and Kirkby Malham.

The Scandinavians left many indications of their settlements in place-names relating to water. O.N. *kelda* 'a spring, well' occurs frequently sometimes as a simplex name, as in Keld, or in compounds like Creskeld 'water-cress' or Halikeld 'holy'. O.N. *mynni* is found in Airmyn, meaning 'mouth of the River Aire', and the dative plural of *bjugr* in Bewholme, in the sense of 'at the bends in the stream'. Beckermonds, a most interesting form, is a compound of O.N. *mot* 'confluence of streams' and the genitive singular *bekkjar* of O.N. *bekkr* 'stream', *mot* being replaced at a later date by -*monds* as a result of the influence of O.Fr. *mont*. Beckermonds is indeed the place where two streams join to form the River Wharfe.

O.N. *bekkr* commonly replaces O.E. *broc* and *burna*. It is found in Ellerbeck (O.N. *elri* 'alder') and Melbecks (O.N. *melr* 'sand-bank') and with a personal-name in Arkle Beck ('Arkil's stream'). Starbeck has no connection with 'stars'; it is derived from O.N. *storr* and means 'a stream where sedge grows'. O.N. *brunnr* is also found for 'stream', sometimes replacing O.E. *burna*, as in Glusburn 'gleaming stream'. In the dative plural it is found in Nunburnholme, meaning 'at the streams', Nun-being a reference to the nunnery there. Other words for 'stream' are *loekr* as in Leake, and *strengr* as in Ellingstring 'Ella's stream'. Skerne is named from Skerne Beck, which is derived from the adjective *skirr* 'bright', probably in the sense of 'cleansing'. O.N. *fors* and *foss*, both meaning 'a waterfall', have developed as *force* and *foss* respectively, as in Thornton Force and Fossdale 'waterfall valley'. Forcett, from *fors* and *saetr*, means 'shieling by the waterfall'. Skipsea, possibly from O.N.

45

saer, may mean 'a lake for ships'. The usual word for a small lake is *tjorn*, as found in such place-names as Malham Tarn, while Thirsk, from O.N. **thresk*, was named from a lake or fen originally found in its vicinity. Thornton Watlass was apparently so named from the lack of water there (O.N. *vatn-lauss* 'waterless'). O.N. *melr* occurs in Rathmel 'red sand-bank'. Unlikely as it seems, it is also found in Meaux; the spelling in *Domesday Book, Melse*, is undoubtedly derived from *melr* and O.E. *sae*, possibly meaning 'lake with sandy shores', but medieval copyists have associated this with *Melsa*, the Latin form of the French abbey at Meaux.

Several words meaning 'marsh' occur. O.N. *kjarr* is frequently found in the simplex name Carr(s), in Sheepscar 'marshy land where sheep graze', Redcar 'red marshy ground' and Ellerker 'a marsh where alders abound'. In Knavesmire 'Knar's marsh' we find O.N. *myrr* 'mire, bog', and also in Ainderby Mires 'Eindrithi's farmstead in the marsh'. Another word for 'marsh' was *marr*, found as a simplex name in Marr. Sowerby (2) and Sowerby Bridge have a first element *saurr*, meaning 'marshy' or 'sour ground'.

Scandinavian words relating to woodland are well represented in Yorkshire place-names. O.N. *skogr* 'a wood' occurs in Thurnscoe, with the meaning of 'thorn-wood', and Aiskew 'oak-wood'. O.N. *storth* 'a plantation' is found as Storiths, Storrs and Storth, and probably in Storwood. The most common element for 'wood' is *vithr*, which occurs in Hartwith 'hart', Menwith 'held in common', Bubwith '*Bubbe' and Tockwith 'Toki'. Two place-names from *hris* 'brushwood' are Ruswarp 'silt-land overgrown with brushwood' and Galtres, where the first element means 'boar'. These animals were prone to lie in brushwood when hunted. Examples of place-names incorporating the names of trees are Askwith 'ash-wood', Askrigg 'ash ridge' and Escrick 'strip of land where ash-trees grow'. Place-names containing O.N. *eiki* 'oak' are mentioned elsewhere. O.N. *buskr* 'a bush' is found in Sedbusk 'bush near the shieling' and Stalling Busk 'the stallions' bush'. The dative plural of O.N. *sneis* 'a twig' is found in Snaizeholme, thirteenth century forms of the name being recorded as *Snaysum*.

Boldron, from O.N. *boli* and *rum*, means 'forest-clearing where steers are kept', while Wetherby, meaning 'wether farm' incorporates O.N. *vethr*. References to horses are found in Rossett Green 'horse wood' and in Hesketh, which means 'horse race-course' (the Scandinavians were keen on horse-racing). O.N. *ikorni* 'a squirrel' occurs in Ickornshaw 'squirrel wood'. The unusual place-name Crackpot does not mean 'an eccentric person'; it is formed from O.N. *kraka* and M.E. *potte* and has the meaning 'ravine frequented by crows'. The second element is commonly found in Yorkshire to describe a deep hole in mountain limestone. O.N. *hrokr* 'rook' is the first element of Rookwith.

Despite the reputation of the Vikings as warriors, they were basically farmers, and in fact were industrious and efficient husbandmen. Many place-names refer to their activities. There are several words to describe pasture, meadows and cultivated land. O.N. *eng* is found in Kettlesing, meaning 'Ketill's water-meadow', and is also the first element of Ingbirch-worth. Muker, formed from O.N. *mjor* and *akr*, means 'a small, unculti-vated field', while the place-name Sleights, of which there are several examples, is derived from O.N. *sletta* 'a level field'. Snape is derived from *snap* 'poor pasturage' and Routh from *hruthr* 'scurf', perhaps in the sense of 'rough ground'. That most peculiar place-name Whaw is derived from O.N. *kvi* and *hagi* and means 'enclosure near the fold'. Another unusual place-name is Thwing, from O.N. *thvengr* 'thong'. This word is cognate with O.E. *thwang* and probably means 'a strip of land' here. Snaith, another oddity, is from *sneith* and means 'a detached piece of ground'. The first element of Crathorne is doubtful, but may be O.N. *kra*, the place-name meaning 'thorn-bush in the nook of land'.

O.N. *garthr* 'enclosure', cognate with O.E. *geard*, which gives Mod.E. *yard*, is found frequently in Yorkshire, especially in field-names. It occurs in Arkengarthdale 'the valley of Arkil's enclosure' and also in Hawsker 'Hawk's enclosure'. O.N. *krokr*, originally meaning 'a bend' but mainly used of 'a nook' or 'a secluded piece of land', is found in Crookes; and *hvarf*, a word of similar meaning, is found in the place-name Wharfe, near Settle, and also in Wharram Percy and Wharram le Street, where it is used to describe the bends in the valley where the villages are situated.

Biggin, a common place-name, is from M.E. *bigging* 'a building', a derivative of *big* 'to build'. O.N. *buth* 'a booth' occurs in Boothroyd 'clearing with a booth', while O.N. *bu* 'a homestead' is probable in Barnbow 'Bjarni's homestead'. The word *hus* 'a house' is the same in Old English and Old Norse, but since the element is common in the Danelaw but rare elsewhere, we may expect use of the Scandinavian word. The following are examples: Blubberhouses, which may have a personal-name 'Bluber' or M.E. *bluber* 'a spring' as a first element; Brighouse means 'houses by the bridge'; Temple Newsam, Newsham (2) and Newsholme all mean '(at) the new houses'; Sykehouse means 'houses by the stream'; Great and Little Moorsholme are '(at) the houses on the moor'; and Howsham is a simplex name from the dative plural *husum*, meaning 'at the houses'. Booze has no connection with intoxicating liquors; it is found in an early form as *Bowehous* and is derived from *boga* and *hus*, with the meaning 'house by the bend', a reference to the shape of a hill nearby.

Another place-name formed from a dative plural is the common Lofthouse (4), together with the variant form Loftus, from O.N. *lopt-hus*, 'a house with a loft'. Birstwith, meaning simply 'a farmstead', is formed from *byjar-stathr*, and Laytham, another dative plural, from *hlatha* 'a barn'. Upsall (2) is from *up-salir* 'high dwellings'. The second element of Stanwick is not O.E. *wic*, but O.N. *veggr*, and the literal meaning is 'stone walls', probably a reference to an old fortification nearby.

There are several Scandinavian words denoting 'mountain pastures' or 'shielings'. During the summer sheep were able to graze higher up the slopes of the Pennines, and it was found convenient to build huts, some-times accommodating two or three people, on the upland pastures for seasonal use. Hence the prevalence in north-western districts of the elements *erg*, *saetr* and *skali*. O.N. *erg*, borrowed from Old Irish, is found in simplex form in Airyholme, Eryholme and Argam 'at the shielings'; as a first element in Arrathorne 'thorn-bush near the shieling'; and as a second element in Feizor 'Fiach's shieling' and Golcar 'Guthlac's shieling'. O.N. *saetr*, with the same meaning, occurs in Appersett 'appletree' and Burtersett 'alder-tree', and with personal-names in Countersett 'Constance', Gunnerside 'Gunnar' and probably in Marsett '*Maurr'. O.N. *skali*, a distinctively Old West Scandinavian word for 'shieling' is found in simplex form as Scale(s) or Scholes. It occurs as a first element in Scaleber 'hill-shieling' and is combined with an O.N. personal-name 'Gamall' in Gammarsgill.

O.E. *geat* and O.N. *gata*, although cognate words, had different meanings; the former was used in place-names to mean 'a gate' or 'a gap' (for example Symonds Yat), while the latter signified 'a way' or 'a road'. There are many examples of the use of *gata*, especially in street-names. It is found in Harrogate, a difficult place-name, which may mean 'road to the cairn' or 'road to Harlow'. The interpretation of Huggate is not certain but it may mean 'road to the mounds'. Ainsty is derived from O.N. *ein-stigi* 'narrow path' and Rastrick from O.N. *rost* and O.E. *ric*, meaning 'a narrow road with a resting-place'. O.N. *vath* is commonly used for 'a ford'. There are several examples of its use in simplex form as Wath (upon Dearne), and one form as Wass. As a second element it usually develops as -*with*, as in Flawith (2), where the first element is uncertain; suggested meanings are 'witch's ford', 'paved ford' and 'ford by the flat meadow-land'. Langwith is simply 'long ford' and Helwith 'a ford made with flat stones'. In Ravensworth 'Hrafn's ford' and Snilesworth 'Snigel's ford', -*wath* has developed as -*worth*. A water-crossing by boat is denoted by O.N. *ferja*. Ferrybridge 'bridge by the ferry' was *Ferie* in *Domesday Book* and remained so until the bridge was built at the end of the twelfth century. Ferry Fryston and North Ferriby are other place-names incorporating 'ferry'.

Most of the examples of place-names given so far in this chapter are wholly of Scandinavian origin, but some are hybrid forms consisting of English and Scandinavian elements. Additionally there are many Yorkshire place-names which although basically English in origin have been subjected to Scandinavian influence. In areas that had not been settled previously, or if so, had been taken over completely by Scandinavians, new place-names of wholly Scandinavian origin were likely. In many areas, however, there would have been a mixed population of English and Scandinavians, and it is here that an Anglo-Scandinavian dialect developed. In these circumstances hybrid names, with English and Scandinavian elements, were formed, or if a place-name of English origin survived, it was often influenced by Scandinavian, through word or sound substitution.

Owing to the similarity of cognate words in the two languages it is not always possible to determine whether a place-name is a true hybrid or whether it is a name that had been subjected to Scandinavian influence. There is, however, one group of place-names, called 'Grimston hybrids', where it is usually possible to be certain about the origin of the constituent elements; these are place-names consisting of a Scandinavian personal-name compounded with O.E. *tun*. Since most of these place-names are found in *Domesday Book*, they most likely refer to places that had been settled quite early. In Yorkshire they are particularly common in the North and East Ridings, where they almost certainly represent the names of English settlements made before the Viking invasions. It is probable that these places had place-names originally consisting of an O.E. personal-name, and *tun*, and after the Viking settlement, for some reason or other, there was substitution of a Scandinavian personal-name. There is some doubt about the reason for such substitutions. It is significant, however, that they lie outside the areas of greatest Scandinavian settlement (that is areas where place-names in *by* predominate) and lie in areas where there was likely to have been a mixed population. Substitution could have occurred when a village had a new Scandinavian owner. Examples of such place-names, which require little comment in themselves, are listed at the end of the chapter. Other hybrid names consist of a Scandinavian personal-name and a final English element other than *tun*, like Addle-brough, from 'Authulfr' and *burh*, and Crakehall from 'Kraki' and *halh*. Again, these are very numerous, and examples are therefore listed at the end of this chapter.

The substitution of a Scandinavian element for an English one occurs extensively in Yorkshire place-names, and usually, but not always, involves the substitution of a cognate word, similar in form and pronunciation. The substitution of O.N. *a* for O.E. *ea* 'river' occurs in Great and Little Ayton and East and West Ayton, and O.N. *hryggr* for O.E. *hrycg* 'ridge' in Reighton and North and East Rigton. O.N. *skor* has replaced O.E. **scor(a)* 'ravine' in Scorton, and *skal* 'hollow' has replaced it in Scawton 'farm in the hollow'. O.N. *steinn* 'stone' is commonly found for O.E. *stan*, as in Stainborough, Stainburn, Staincliffe, Stainforth, Stainland, North and South Stainley, Stainmore and Stainton.

Marton, Marton in Cleveland, Marton in the Forest and Marton le Moor have O.N. *marr* 'marsh' for O.E. *mere*. Scandinavian first elements have replaced English words in Hatfield and Great and Little Hatfield 'heath-land' and Howden 'valley by the headland'. O.N. *geiri* has replaced O.E. *gara* 'a triangular piece of land' in Garforth (*ford*) and Gargrave (*graf* 'grove'). O.N. *skarth* 'gap' has replaced O.E. *sceard* in Scarcroft, although its precise significance is not clear. In Watton, from O.E. *waet* and *dun*, meaning 'wet hillside', we have the substitution of O.N. *vatr* for *waet*. In Carlton, a very common place-name in York-shire, meaning 'village of the free peasants', O.E. *ceorl* has been replaced by the cognate O.N. *karl*. In Conisbrough, Coniston Cold and Coni-stone, O.E. *cyning* 'king' has been replaced by O.N. *konungr*.

Many place-names incorporating tree-names show substitution. There are Scandinavian words for English words in Ackton and Aughton 'oak',

Ellerton Abbey, Ellerton Priory and Ellerton on Swale 'alder', Askern, Askham Bryan and Askham Richard 'ash' and Almsford Bridge 'elm'. Hazlewood, Hessay and Hessle (2) show the Scandinavian form of 'hazel' and Humbleton has O.N. *humli* 'hop' for O.E. *humele*. Sproxton incoporates an Old Danish word for 'brushwood'. In Kirk Bramwith 'broom wood', O.E. *wudu* has been replaced by O.N. *vithr*, with the same meaning. Beckwithshaw provides a good example of a tautological place-name. The original form was *Bec-wudu* 'beech-wood', but O.N. *bekkr* and *vithr* replaced the original name, and then O.E. *sceaga*, also meaning 'wood', was added for good measure. O.N. *stutr* 'bullock' is possibly found in Sutton and *geit* 'she-goat' in Gateforth. O.N. *drag* 'portage' has been substituted for O.E. *draeg* in Draughton, and also in Drax. Spaunton has the O.N. word *spann*, meaning 'shingle roof'.

Substitution of words denoting position was frequent. Owston, Austwick and Owstwick all derive from O.N. *austr* 'east', and Malton, Melbourne, Melton, High Melton, West Melton and Methley from *methal* 'middle'. O.N. *nezti* 'lowest' has been substituted in Nesfield. Brayton and Braithwell have O.N. *breithr* for O.E. *brad* 'broad'. O.N. *rauthr* 'red' commonly replaces O.E. *read* as in Rawcliff, Rawcliffe (2), Roecliffe, Rawdon (with *dun* 'hill'), Rawmarsh and Roppa 'red path.' The substitution of O.N. *kirkja* 'church' for O.E. *cirice* was referred to in the last chapter.

Substitution has not always been one way, however, and there are examples of Scandinavian words being replaced by English words. The original form of Scarborough suggests that it was a combination of *skogr* and *both* 'a booth in a wood', but *both* was replaced by *burh* after the Conquest when a castle was built there. In some examples of the place-name Newby, no doubt O.E. *niwe* replaced O.N. *nyr*, and in formations containing O.N. *askr* 'ash', substitution of O.E. *aesc* has occurred. Stonegrave has an early spelling from O.N. *steinn*. In Shunner Howe an original *sj* (O.N. 'Sjonr') has become *sh*. Early forms of East Riding as *Austriding(e)* or *Oustridinge* show that O.E. *east* has ultimately prevailed. In Cleckheaton, O.E. *heah* and *tun*, meaning 'high farmstead', have been retained, but O.N. *klakkr* 'hill' has been added.

It is often difficult to decide whether a place-name contains an English or Scandinavian element since many pairs of words are so alike that it is impossible to distinguish between them. Examples of such pairs, with the Old English word first, are: *beorg/berg* 'hill', *boga/bogi* 'bend', *calf/kalfr* 'calf', *clif/klif* 'cliff, bank', *dael/dalr* 'valley', *fola/foli* 'foal', *galga/galgi* 'gallows', *hafoc/haukr* 'hawk', *hraefn/hrafn* 'raven', *hroc/hrokr* 'rook', *mos/mosi* 'bog' and *swin/svin* 'swine'. It may usually be assumed that the Scandinavian form has been used in the Danelaw if use of the Old English form is rare in other parts of the country. Scandinavian origin is also probable if the other elements in the place-name are Scandinavian.

Sound substitution occurred where Scandinavian speakers were unfamiliar with sounds in Old English words and substituted sounds found in Scandinavian. One of the most common was the substitution of

Scandinavian *sk* for English *sc*. By the time of the Scandinavian invasions the consonants *sc* in Old English were pronounced as *sh*, but were preserved as *sk* in Scandinavian (words that show the two developments are the doublets[1] Mod.E. *shirt/skirt* and *shrub/scrub*). In place-names *sc* was pronounced *sk* in areas of Scandinavian settlement, and so we have place-names like Skipton and Skipton upon Swale, from O.Nb. *scip* and O.E. *tun*, meaning 'sheep village', pronounced and spelt with *sk* as against the Old English form Shipton. There is similar sound substitution in Skibeden (identical to Shibden) 'sheep valley', Skipwith 'sheep wood' and Skiplam '(at) the cowsheds'. Skyrack has similarly developed from O.E. *scir-ac* 'shire oak' and Minskip from O.E. (*ge*)*maenscipe* 'a place held communally'. O.E. *scir* also meant 'bright', and is found in this sense, pronounced as *sk* in Skircoat (with O.E. *cot* 'cottage') and North and South Skirlaugh (with O.E. *leah* 'clearing'). In West Scrafton 'tun in a hollow', and Scriven 'place at a hollow', perhaps a reference to gravel pits in the locality, O.E. *scraef* 'pit' has become subject to Scandinavian influence. Aske, meaning 'ash-tree', and Scackleton, from *denu* not *tun*, perhaps meaning 'a valley marked by a pole', show similar influence. O.E. *scelf*, meaning 'a bank' or 'shelving terrain' may be the first element of Skelton *frequently* 'tun on a shelf of land', and the second element of Raskelf 'a shelf of land frequented by roe-bucks', Hinderskelfe 'Hildr's shelf of land' and Ulleskelf 'Ulfr's shelf of land', with the substitution of *sk* for *sc*, although there is the possibility in some or all of these place-names that O.N. *skjalf* is the original element.

Another type of sound substitution arose from the fact that O.E. *c* was pronounced *ch* before a front vowel, although the spelling was retained, while *k* was preserved in Scandinavian. Thus we have the place-names East Keswick and Dunkeswick, from O.E. *cese* and *wic*, with the meaning of 'cheese-farm', while outside the Danelaw the development would have given Cheswick or Chiswick. Scandinavian influence similarly accounts for the initial *k* in such place-names as Kelfield and Great and Little Kelk (from O.E. **celc* 'chalk', a reference to the soil), Kellington ('Ceolla' and *tun*), Kettlewell 'bubbling stream', Kildwick 'dairy-farm of the young men', Kilpin 'calf enclosure' (from O.E. *celf*, another form of *calf*), Kilton 'farmstead of the young men' and Kippax '**Cippa's ash-tree*'.

The consonant *d* was pronounced *th* between vowels in Scandinavian so the twelfth century form *Godeland* 'Goda's land' developed into Goathland. Other place-names similarly influenced are Clotherholme (dative plural of O.E. **cluder* 'at the rocks'), Lothersdale ('the beggar's valley') from O.E. *loddere* and O.N. *dalr* replacing O.E. *denu*, and Hotham (dative plural of O.E. **hod* 'at the shelters'). Initial O.E. *g* was softened and became *y* while in Scandinavian *g* was preserved; this accounts for the hard *g* sound in Giggleswick and Gilling. In Scandinavian initial *w* was lost; this explains forms like Ovington, where 'Wulfa' has been influenced by O.N. 'Ulfr' and Ulrome, from O.E. '*Wulfhere' and *ham*.

---

[1] Doublets means one of a pair, especially one of two words of the same derivation but different sense.

Several facets of Scandinavian administrative and social organisation are revealed in place-names. The Shire of York, established some time after the Viking invasions, was further divided into the East, North and West Ridings, so named from O.N. *thrithjungr* 'a third part', which survived as administrative units until a few years ago. The three Ridings were divided into wapentakes, the equivalent of the English hundred, nearly all the wapentake names, like Buckrose, Ewcross, Osgoldcross, Halikeld, Agbrigg, and the like, being of Scandinavian origin. O.N. *vapnatak* literally means 'brandishing of spears', this originally being the sign of approval to confirm a decision at a tribal council. In some parts of Yorkshire there was a division into bierlaws or byrlaws, as exemplified by place-names like Brampton Bierlow, Brightside Bierlow and Ecclesfield Bierlow. The name is derived from O.N. *byjar-log* 'the law of the village' but the word was used in the sense of 'township'. O.N. *thing* 'assembly council' is found in Tingley 'mound where the council was held', which may have been the meeting-place of Morley Wapentake, while in Laughton en le Morthen and Brampton en le Morthen we have *mor-thing* 'assembly of (the people) of the moors'. Gildersome, from the dative plural of O.N. *gildi-hus* 'guild-house', shows the existence of guilds in some form, while Wetwang may be derived from a legal term, O.N. *vaett-vangr*, meaning 'a place to which parties to a dispute are summoned'.

Some place-names refer to aspects of Scandinavian social organisation. O.N. *drengr* is found in Dringhouses 'houses of the drengs' and Dringhoe 'a hill held by a dreng' and refers to a person holding land by free tenure. In Lazenby we have the term *leysingi* 'a freedman'. Holderness takes its name from *holdr* 'a higher yeoman' and *naess* or *nes* 'a headland'. Almondbury, from O.N. *al-menn* and O.E. *burh*, means 'a fortified place owned by all the men', that is the men of the village.

Although few details are known about the conversion of the Scandinavians to Christianity, this most probably occurred shortly after the date of settlement. As we have seen O.N. *kirkja* replaced O.E. *cirice* in place-names. Mod.E. *cross* is derived from O.Ir. *cros*, a word brought to England by the Norwegians and this is found in several Yorkshire place-names, including South Crosland 'tract of land where a cross is situated', Ewcross, Osgoldcross and Staincross Wapentakes, Thruscross 'Thori's cross', etcetera.

There are few references to heathen worship, although there may be a relic in the word *lundr*, meaning 'a wood' but earlier 'a sacred grove', and found in Lund(s), Lumby and Swanland 'Svanr's wood'. There may conceivably be a reference to the god Odin in Roseberry Topping, since an early form of the place-name is *Othenesberg*, and so this well-known landmark may have been a place where Odin was worshipped. A reference to Scandinavian mythology is found in Trollers Gill, from O.N. *troll* and O.E. *ears*, literally 'the troll's arse', probably so named from the topographical features of the place.

Few monuments or inscriptions survive to show the extent to which the Scandinavian language continued to be spoken in Yorkshire, but there are some linguistic features in place-names pointing to its survival. Although English was spoken at the court of King Cnut, a complete fusion of the two languages in an area of such intensive Scandinavian settlement as Yorkshire is hardly likely to have occurred until long after the Norman Conquest.

Place-names containing personal-names are:—

by (O.N.):

Ainderby (3) 'Eindrithi', Aislaby (Pickering) 'Aslakr', Aislaby (Whitby) 'Asulfr', Amotherby 'Oymundr', Anlaby 'Anlaf' (Anglo-Scandinavian), Asenby 'Oysteinn', Asselby 'Askell', Bagby 'Baggi', Balby 'Balli', Barmby on the Marsh and Barmby on the Moor 'Barne', Barnby and Barnby Dun 'Bjarni', Belby 'Belli', Bellerby 'Belgr', Bessingby 'Bes(s)ingr', Bielby 'Beli', Boltby 'Boltr', Brandsby 'Brandr', Brawby 'Bragi', Great and Little Busby '*Buski', Cadeby 'Kati', Carnaby '*Keyrandi', Cleasby '*Kless', Cowesby 'Kausi', Easby (2) 'Esi', Exelby 'Eskel', Faceby '*Feitr', Firby (2) 'Frithi', Flasby and Flaxby 'Flatr', Fockerby 'Folkvarthr', Garrowby 'Gervardh', Gilmonby '*Gilmathr', Girsby 'Griss', Haldenby 'Halfdanr', Harmby 'Hjaerne', Hawnby 'Halmi', Haxby 'Hakr', Helperby 'Hjalpr' (feminine), Holtby 'Holti', Hornby (Catterick) 'Horni', Hornby (Great Smeaton) '*Hornbothi', Cold Kirby and Kearby 'Kaerir', Maltby (2) 'Malti', Maunby 'Magni', Milby 'Mildi', Ormesby 'Ormr', Osgodby 'Asgautr', Rokeby 'Hrokr', Romanby 'Hromundr', Roxby (2) 'Rauthr', Hutton Rudby and Rudby 'Rudi', Scalby (2) 'Skalli', Sewerby 'Siward', Sinderby 'Sindri', Skeeby 'Skithi', Skidby 'Skyti', Slingsby '*Slengr', Swainby 'Sveinn', Thimbleby '*Thymill', Thirkleby (2) 'Thorkell', Thirlby '*Thrylli', Thirtleby 'Thorkell', Thoralby 'Thorvaldr', Thoresby 'Thorr', Thorganby 'Thorgrimr', Thormanby and Thornaby 'Thormothr', Uckerby '*Utkari', Uncleby '*Hunkell', Whitby 'Hviti'.

(O.E.):

Baldersby 'B(e)aldhere', Ellerby (2) 'Aelfweard', Warlaby 'Waerlaf', Willerby (2) 'Wilheard'.

thorp (O.N.):

Allerthorpe 'Alfvarthr', Bowthorpe 'Bulle', Boythorpe 'Boie', Bugthorpe 'Buggi', Burythorpe 'Bjorg' (feminine), Carthorpe and Caythorpe 'Kari', Foggathorpe 'Folkvarthr', Fraisthorpe '*Freistingr', Fridaythorpe possibly '*Frjadagr', Ganthorpe 'Galmr', Gribthorpe 'Gripr', Grimthorpe 'Grimr', Gristhorpe 'Griss', Haisthorpe '*Haskell', Harlthorpe '*Herle', Helperthorpe 'Hjalpr' (feminine), Hilderthorpe 'Hildigar', Ingerthorpe 'Ingirithr', Kelleythorpe '*Kel(l)ingr', Kennythorpe '*Kennari', Langthorpe (earlier *Langlivetorp*) 'Langlifr' (feminine), Lowthorpe 'Lagi', Menethorpe '*Menningr', Menthorpe 'Menni' or 'Menja' (feminine), Ousethorpe 'Ulfr', Raisthorpe 'Hreitharr', Scagglethorpe 'Skokull', Scosthrop 'Skoltr', Skelmanthorpe 'Skjaldmarr', Tholthorpe

'Thorolfr', Tibthorpe 'Tibbi', Towthorpe (2) 'Tofi', Ugthorpe 'Uggi', Weaverthorpe 'Vithfari', Wilstrop 'Vifill', Youlthorpe 'Eyjolfr'.

(O.E.):

Eddlethorpe 'Eadwald', Kingthorpe 'Cyna', Osmondthorpe 'Osmund'. Armthorpe O.E. 'Earnwulf' or O.Dan. 'Arnwulf', Cowthorpe O.E. 'Cola' or O.N. 'Koli'.

hybrid *tun:*

Barkston 'Barkr', Brotherton 'Brothir', Burneston and Burniston 'Bryningr', Elloughton possibly 'Helgi', Flockton and Folkton 'Folki', Foston, Foston on the Wolds and Fewston 'Fotr', Fryton 'Frithi', Ganton 'Galmr', Garriston 'Gjartharr', Grimston *frequently*, North Grimston and Hanging Grimston 'Grimr', Hilston 'Hildulfr', Moulton and Muston 'Musi', Nafferton 'Nattfari', Nawton 'Nagli', Oulston 'Ulfr', Royston and Ruston Parva 'Roarr', Scampston 'Skammr', Scruton 'Skurfa', Kirby Sigston 'Siggr', Sneaton 'Snjo', Staxton 'Stakkr', Thurlstone 'Thorulfr', Towton 'Tofi', Wigginton 'Vikingr', Youlton 'Joli'.

other hybrids:

burh Addlebrough 'Authulfr', Barnburgh 'Bjarni', Flamborough 'Fleinn', Guisborough 'Gigr', Hemingbrough 'Hemingr', Kexbrough 'Keptr', Londesborough 'Lethinn', Scarborough 'Skarthi'; *burhtun* Brandesburton 'Brandr', Humberton 'Hundr'; *clif* Felliscliffe 'Felagr'; *cot* Muscoates 'Musi'; *dael* Kirby Underdale 'Hundolfr'; *denu* Erringden 'Eirikr', Scammonden 'Skammbeinn'; *feld* Hellifield 'Helgi'; *ford* Birdforth 'Bruthr'; *foss* Fangfoss 'Fangulf'; *fleot* Yokefleet 'Jokell'; *halh* Crakehall 'Kraki', Hensall 'Hethinn', Odsal 'Oddr'; *ing* Skeckling 'Skakle', Skeffling 'Skapti'; *ingaham* Scrayingham 'Skra'; *land* Barkisland 'Barki', Thurgoland 'Thorgeirr', Thurstonland 'Thorsteinn'; *leah* Azerley 'Atsurr', Osmotherley 'Asmundr', Wickersley 'Vikarr'; *thorn* Sigglesthorne 'Sigolfr'; *wella* Bracewell 'Breithr'; *worth* Brodsworth 'Broddr'; *wic* Beswick 'Bessi', Burstwick 'Bursti', Hawkswick 'Haukr', Kepwick 'Kaeppi'.

7.   Later Developments

AFTER the Norman Conquest the language of the new ruling class, Norman French, became the official and literary language of England, and the close contacts that were maintained with France for several centuries helped to keep it in a position of dominance. Latin, too, was an important language in official, as well as ecclesiastical, circles. English, however, continued to be spoken by the mass of the people and ultimately emerged as the dominant language (Parliament was first opened in English in 1362), although by then it had a strong admixture of French words. So far as Yorkshire place-names are concerned, French influence is small, and apart from a few new names of French origin, is largely confined to spelling.

Since the Normans were great builders of castles and founders of monasteries French names were given to these places. O.Fr. *mont* 'a hill, mount' was an element in common use, and in Yorkshire we find it, with O.Fr. *riche* 'strong', in Richmond. The use of O.Fr. *castel* as an affix in such place-names as Scarborough Castle, Castle Bolton and Hardcastle, needs no emphasising. In Castleford *castel* has replaced O.E. *ceaster*, the original form of the name being *Casterford*, and perhaps this has also occurred in Castley, meaning 'clearing by the fortification'. Pontefract, the site of another Norman castle, was originally from Latin *pons fractus* 'broken bridge', which became O.Fr. *pont freit*, giving the modern form Pomfret. Pontefract is therefore a spelling pronunciation.

In Fountains Abbey, from O.Fr. *fontein*, there is a reference to the springs found there. Fountains Earth (probably from O.E. *eorthe* in the sense of 'a tract of land') and Fountains Fell, both take their name from the abbey. Grosmont and Mount Grace provide additional examples of forms arising from O.Fr. *mont*, while Haltemprice, from O.Fr. *haute emprise* 'great enterprise' is a reference to an Augustinian priory in the locality. O.Fr. *vals* occurs in Rieuvaulx, meaning 'valley of the Rye', and also in Jervaulx 'valley of the Ure'. The element is found as *vale* in the Vale of Pickering and the Vale of York.

There are a few other Yorkshire place-names formed from O.Fr. words or showing French influence. Balne is probably from O.Fr. *balne* 'bathing-place'. O.Fr. *chapel*, as in Chapel Allerton, is commonly found. M.E. *goule* 'ditch', from an O.Fr. word originally, is found in Goole, while the first element of Grewelthorpe is possibly from O.Fr. *gruel*, the place-name perhaps meaning 'a farmstead owned by a miller'. O.Fr. *mal* 'bad' occurs in Malpas 'difficult passage' and with *assart* in Kirkby Malzeard 'poor clearing'. Laund from O.Fr. *launde* 'forest-glade' is commonly found, especially in minor names. Roche, meaning 'rock', is from O.Fr. *roche*, and the unusual place-name Tilts is probably from O.Fr. *til* 'lime-tree'. Roundhay is a hybrid name, formed from O.Fr. *rond* and O.E. *(ge)haeg*, and means 'round enclosure', probably in the sense of one used for hunting.

Numerous examples of O.Fr. *le* occur, as in Hutton le Hole, Newton le Willows, etcetera. Originally *en le* occurred in such forms, but *en* usually disappeared, although it remains in Brampton en le Morthen and Laughton en le Morthen.

Old French personal-names are rarely found, but there are examples in Countersett 'Constance', Huby (Otley) 'Hugo' and Jolby 'Johel'. Lupset may possibly be derived from a M.E. by-name 'Lupe' from O.Fr. *loup* 'wolf', the second element being O.E. *heafod*, perhaps in the sense of 'hill'.

French influence on Yorkshire place-names is also to be seen in the use of feudal affixes. The name of the family holding the manor was commonly used as an affix, particularly where it was found necessary to distinguish between two places of the same name, and so place-names like Acaster Malbis, Farnley Tyas, and the like, arose. Occasionally such a family name is of English or Scandinavian origin. If possession of the manor had been given to an official, the affix might denote his rank, as in place-names like Constable Burton, Sheriff Hutton, Thornton Steward, and so on. Place-names with an affix are too numerous to list in the text, and are therefore given at the end of the chapter.

Many other French words found their way into English and some of them became common elements in later place-names, expecially minor ones. The meaning of these O.Fr. forms is usually evident, but in the select list that follows, the Mod.E. equivalent is shown where necessary: *chace* 'chase', *clos* 'close', *conduit*, *copeiz* 'coppice', *crois* 'cross', *forest*, *grange*, *loge* 'lodge', *market*, *mote* 'moat', *park*, *paroche* 'parish', *pasture*, *place*, *plain*, *quarriere* 'quarry', *rail(e)* 'rail' or 'fence', *raton* 'rat, rat-infested', *tour* 'tower' and *wareine* 'warren'.

There was some French influence on the spelling and pronunciation of existing English place-names. Since spelling was not fixed (it only became fixed as a result of the influence of printing-houses during the seventeenth and eighteenth centuries) and was an attempt to represent sounds phonetically, it was only natural that, in documents written and copied by scribes who were Anglo-Norman and Latin speakers, sounds and combinations of letters that were unfamiliar to them should be replaced by sounds they knew.

Such influence accounts for the different developments of O.E. *ceaster*, from Latin *castra*. In Yorkshire *-caster* generally remained, as shown by forms like Doncaster and Tadcaster, but in most parts of the country since O.E. *c* became *ch* before front vowels, forms like Chester and Colchester arise. Anglo-Norman speakers, however, pronounced *ch* as *ts* and then as *s*, and so we have forms like Gloucester and Cirencester. Another type of change is exemplified by the place-name Dishforth, where O.E. *dic*, normally developing into *dike*, became Dish- owing to French influence. Similarly, Anglo-Norman speakers found difficulty in pronouncing *th*, and pronounced this initially as *t*. Thus *Thorp* is generally written as *Torp* in *Domesday Book*. Tankersley 'Thancred's clearing' provides an example of the change. Initial *y* was pronounced as *j* by Anglo-Norman speakers, and this accounts for the modern pronunciation of Jervaulx (from *Yorevallis*). Initial *sh* was pronounced as *s* and so we have Over and Nether Silton and Silpho from O.E. *scylf*, a variant of *shelf* 'shelving terrain'.

There have been few new place-names in modern times. The villages of Middle, Nether and Over Shitlington, meaning 'Scyttel's farmstead', had their names changed to Middlestown, Netherton and Overton respectively, for obvious reasons. Likewise Shuttleworth, from O.E. *scytels* 'a bar, pole' and *worth*, meaning 'an enclosure closed by means of a bar', was changed to Littleworth. The village of Boston Spa was an eighteenth-century creation, so named after a mineral spring had been discovered there. Ben Rhydding took its name from the Hydro there, the first of its kind in the country, established in 1844. Saltaire was named in 1853 after Sir Titus Salt, who moved his mills there from Bradford and also built houses nearby for his workers and their families. Queensbury, formerly known by the name of its inn, the *Queen's Head*, was so re-named by a decision made at a public meeting in 1863. Triangle also took its name from an inn, the *Triangle Inn*, so called from its situation on a triangular piece of ground. The place-name Smelthouses is also comparatively recent, the allusion being to smelting that was carried on there. A twentieth-century creation is the place-name Dormanstown, an estate built near Middlesbrough in 1918 and named after its builders, Dorman Long.

The following is a list of place-names with feudal affixes, most of which are of French origin:

Acaster Malbis, Appleton Roebuck, Askham Bryan, Askham Richard, Allerton Mauleverer, Bank Newton, Bolton Percy, Burton Agnes, Burton Constable, Burton Fleming, Burton Salmon, Constable Burton, Carlton Miniott, Farnley Tyas, Hirst Courtney, Hooton Levitt, Hooton Pagnell, Hooton Roberts, Hutton Bonville, Hutton Bushell, Hutton Conyers, Kilnwick Percy, Middleton Tyas, Newton Kyme, Newton Morell, Norton Conyers, Purston Jaglin, Seaton Ross, Sheriff Hutton, Studley Roger, Studley Royal, Thornton Rust, Thornton Steward, Thorp Arch, Thorpe Audlin, Thorpe Bassett, Thorpe Lidgett, Thorp Perrow, Thorpe Salvin, Thorpe Stapleton, Thorpe Willoughby, Walden Stubbs, Wharram Percy.

Feudal names also occur in Pinchinthorpe 'Pinchun' and Thorngumbald 'Gumbald'.

8. Street-Names and Minor Names

MANY street-names in Yorkshire's ancient towns and cities were established in the Middle Ages, while in York some even date from the ninth and tenth centuries when the city was the capital of a Scandinavian kingdom. Although many old street-names have disappeared in the course of time owing to road widening and rebuilding, those that have survived are sufficiently numerous and diverse for far more to be written about them than is possible in this book. The short survey that follows is therefore highly selective, but it is hoped that the reader will wish to pursue the subject further on his own account.

In Yorkshire's towns and cities the word often used to denote a street is *gate* from O.N. *gata*, but we also find *street, lane, bar*, etcetera. High Street is commonly found to describe the principal street of a town. Other generally descriptive names are Micklegate, denoting size, and such names as Coney Street (from O.N. *konungr* 'king') and Aldwark ('old fortification'), all in York. To denote location we have the frequent Northgate, Eastgate, Southgate and Westgate. Paved streets are named in Stonegate and The Pavement, both in York, and marshy, dirty conditions are indicated in Marsh Gate (Doncaster), Cargate (York), Lurk Lane and Keldgate (Beverley). Finkle Street, of which there are examples in Hull, Knaresborough, Thirsk, York and other places, is derived from an Old Danish word meaning 'angle' and indicates that the street is at a right angle to another one, usually a main street.

In some street-names, which give directions, the words 'leading to' are implied. Thus Moorgate (Beverley) means 'street leading to the moor' and Boroughgate (Otley) 'street leading to the town'. Similar names are Briggate (Knaresborough, Leeds) 'bridge', Castlegate (Knaresborough, York) 'castle', Gallowgate (Richmond) 'gallows', Gibbet Street (Halifax) 'gibbet', and Lairgate (Beverley) and Laithgate (Doncaster), both from *hlatha* 'barn'. Fossgate, Ousegate and Water Lane, all in York, are of a similar type. In York, also, are King's Staith and Queen's Staith, which are landing-stages on the Ouse.

Many streets are named because of their proximity to churches. Thus York has Gillygate 'St. Giles' (although the church no longer stands there), Marygate 'St. Mary's Abbey', Petergate 'St. Peter's' (the Minster) and St. Saviourgate 'St. Saviour's'. Kirkgate 'the street leading to the church' is a common street-name, and we also have Vicar Lane in Beverley and Leeds. The interesting names, The Bedern (York) and Bedern Bank

58

(Ripon), mean 'the prayer-house' and are derived from O.E. *bed-aern*. Several streets are named after monks or friars, for example Monkgate (York) and Blackfriarsgate and Whitefriarsgate (Hull).

Some streets indicate the nationality of the people living there; hence Flemingate (Beverley), Frenchgate (Richmond and Doncaster), and Jewbury 'the Jews' quarter' and Jubbergate 'street of the Jews' in York. There are several names from O.N. *bondi* 'free-peasant', although by the time such streets were named, the meaning had probably changed to 'bondman, serf'. Bond End (Knaresborough), Bondgate (Otley) and Bondgate Green (Ripon) are examples. Goodramgate (York) is derived from a personal-name 'Guthrum'.

Street-names that show animals were kept there or led along there occur frequently. Hengate 'hens' is found in Beverley, Hungate 'hounds' in York, and there are the self-explanatory names Swinegate and Boar Lane in Leeds and Sheep Street in Skipton. The Bull Ring 'the place where bulls are baited' is found in Beverley, and Flowergate, meaning '(at) the cow stalls' from *florum*, dative plural of O.N. *florr*, is found in Whitby.

References to the street where the market was held are numerous. Thus we have the common Market Place or Market Street, Cheapside in Knaresborough and Wakefield, and the unusual names Wednesday Market and Saturday Market in Beverley. In York St. Sampson's Square is the place where the lost *Thursday Market* was situated. Bootham 'at the shelters', dative plural of O.N. *buth*, in York, was the place where the monks and friars of St. Mary's Abbey had the right to hold a market. Streets were often named after the commodities that were sold there. Bread Street is found in Wakefield and Bargate Street 'the street along which barley was led' is found in Richmond. The Shambles, York's famous street, and also the lost name of a street in Leeds, is derived from O.E. *sceamol* 'bench' and refers to the benches used for the sale of meat.

In mediaeval times specialists in particular trades tended to occupy the same street or quarter, and so many street-names denote occupations. Baxter Gate in Doncaster was 'the street of the bakers', while *Beggargate Lane*, in York, now lost, was 'the street of the bagmakers'. Blossomgate in Ripon and Blossom Street in York were streets where ploughmen lived (from O.N. *plog-sveinn* 'ploughman'). Again in York, Colliergate was 'the (char)coal dealers' street', Coppergate 'the joiners' street' and Felter Lane 'the lane where the feltmakers live'. Fishergate, found in Doncaster, Ripon and York, was 'the fishermen's street'; and in York, Skeldergate was 'the street of the shield-makers' and Spurriergate 'the street of the spur-makers'.

A few street-names refer to wool manufacture. Blake Street (York) may refer to the process of bleaching, while Woolshops in Halifax was a place where wool was sold. Walkergate in Beverley and Otley means 'street of the cloth-fullers', and Tentergate in Knaresborough was a street where cloth was stretched on tenters.

Grape Lane (York) and Mabgate (Leeds), the first element of the latter meaning 'a loose woman', were possibly streets of ill-repute, while Hustlergate in Bradford was probably a street frequented by pickpockets.

To conclude this short survey a few unusual street-names might be mentioned. In Ripon a street, now lost, named from O.E. *bere* and *ford* and meaning 'a ford used for carrying barley' became *Barefoot Street* due to folk etymology. Also in Ripon is Borrage Green, from M.E. *burgage* 'a freehold property in the town'. The Calls in Leeds is of uncertain meaning; it may mean 'a street along which cattle are driven' or it may refer to a weir on the River Aire. The Land of Green Ginger in Hull may possibly take its name from the ginger plant, the root of which is used as a preserve. Again in Hull is Rotten Herring Staith, which has no connection with bad fish, but is named from the family of John Rotenhering. The unusual name Toll Gavel, found in Beverley, means 'a place where tolls are collected'. The Wicker in Sheffield may be from O.N. **vikir* 'willow-tree'. Last but not least there is the most famous street-name of all—York's Whip-ma Whop-ma Gate, which may be named after a whipping post and pillory formerly located at the end of the street, although this meaning is by no means certain.

The derivation of some minor names may be of interest to those who are familiar with the topography of the Yorkshire Dales. That conspicuous landmark, Almscliff Crag, is found as *Almuseclyue* in the thirteenth century, and may be derived from a feminine personal-name '**Almus*', perhaps of Scandinavian origin. Birk Crag is from O.N. *birki* 'birch' and Brimham, as in Brimham Rocks, is derived from an early form *Bernebeam*, from 'Byrna' and *beam* 'tree'. The Cow and Calf Rocks at Ilkley denote a large and a small rock (compare this with the River Riccal which means 'calf of'). Whernside, from O.E. *cweorn-side*, means 'a hill where millstones are obtained'.

Dibble Bridge, near Guisborough, means 'the bridge near the deep pool', from O.E. *deop* and O.N. *hylr*, while Dibble's Bridge, on the Pateley Bridge-Grassington road, also has this meaning, but is derived from O.E. **dybb* (with suffix *-el*). The bridge crosses the River Dibb, which has probably been named from Dibble. O.E. *dogga* is found in Dob Park, near Leathley. Gordale Scar takes its name from O.E./O.N. *gor* 'dirt, dung' and *dael* 'valley'.

Hack Fall, from O.E. *haca* 'hook, bend' and *(ge)fall* 'clearing' may refer to the bends of the River Ure there. The name Haddockstones, near Markington, is obscure, but may mean 'Hadduc's stones', while Haddock Stone, near Farnley, has a different etymology and means 'a heap of loose stones'. Heber's Ghyll, Ilkley, is named from a local family called Heber. How Stean, in the upper part of Nidderdale, is from O.E. *hol* 'a hole, hollow' and *stan* 'stone'.

Ivelet, in Swaledale, means 'Ifa's slope' and Kidstone Pass, in Wharfedale, is derived from M.E. *kide* 'kid' (compare this with Deer Stones from O.E. *deor* 'animal, deer'). The etymology of Mastiles Lane, near Kilnsey, is uncertain, but may be from O.E. *mersc* 'marsh' and *stigel* 'stile'. Norber simply means 'north hill' from *north* and *beorg*. Penny Pot Lane, near Harrogate, may be so named from a nearby house where ale was sold at a penny a pot. O.Fr. *raton* 'rat-infested' occurs in Ratten Gill, near Glus-burn, while Riffa Wood, near Pool in Wharfedale, may be from O.N. *refr* 'a fox'. Rombald's Moor takes its name from an Old German personal-name 'Rumbald'.

Skip Bridge, situated on the Harrogate-York road where it crosses the River Nidd, may be derived from O.Nb. *scip* 'sheep' or O.N. *skoyti* 'winding' (the road curves at this point). The celebrated Strays at Harro-gate are derived from M.E. *stray* 'a piece of unenclosed ground'. Simon's Seat and Earl's Seat are both from O.N. *saeti*, meaning 'a seat' or 'an outcrop of rock in the form of a seat'. O.E. *stride* 'a stride, a place that can be stridden over' is the meaning of the Strid. Stump Cross, a common minor name in Yorkshire, is from O.E. *stubb* 'a stump', the reference being to the broken remains of a cross.

The foregoing are but a few of the minor place-names to be found in Yorkshire. A glance at any Ordnance Survey map relating to the county will reveal many more that stimulate our interest and curiosity. Much of the early history of the Yorkshire landscape is, in fact, to be discovered through its place-names, and their study, together with that of field-names, which are numbered in thousands and which have not even been touched upon in this book, is of immense importance to the local historian. For those who wish to learn more about the subject, recourse to the volumes of the survey by the English Place-Name Society, which are to be found in most town reference libraries, is essential. The single volumes on the place-names of the North Riding and the East Riding, both by Professor A. H. Smith, provide early spellings and etymologies of all the principal and of many minor place-names, while the later monumental work in eight volumes on the West Riding, by the same author, is a com-prehensive study of all its place- and field-names.

Select Bibliography

General Works

R. G. Collingwood and J. N. L. Myers, *Roman Britain and the English Settlements*, 2nd edition, Oxford, 1937.

K. Jackson, *Language and History in Early Britain*, Edinburgh, 1953.

F. M. Stenton, *Anglo-Saxon England*, 3rd edition, Oxford, 1971.

General Works on Place-Names

K. Cameron, *English Place-Names*, 3rd edition, London, 1977.

G. J. Copley, *English Place-Names and their Origins*, London, 1968.

E. Ekwall, *The Concise Oxford Dictionary of English Place-Names*, 4th edition, Oxford, 1960.

M. Gelling, *Signposts to the Past*, London ,1978.

P. H. Reaney, *The Origin of English Place-Names*, London, 1960.

A. H. Smith, English Place-Name Society, Vols. XXV & XXVI. *English Place-Name Elements*, Pts. I & II, Cambridge, 1956.

Works on Yorkshire Place-Names

G. Fellows Jensen, *Scandinavian Settlement-Names in Yorkshire*, Copenhagen, 1972.

A. H. Smith, English Place-Name Society, Vol. V. *The North Riding of Yorkshire*, Cambridge, 1928.

A. H. Smith, English Place-Name Society, Vol. XIV. *The East Riding of Yorkshire and York*, Cambridge, 1937.

A. H. Smith, English Place-Name Society, Vols. XXX-XXXVII. *The West Riding of Yorkshire*, Pts. I-VIII, Cambridge, 1962.

Index

Fossdale, 45.
Fossgate, 58.
Foston, 54.
Foston on the Wolds, 36, 54.
Fountains Abbey, 55.
Fountains Earth, 55.
Fountains Fell, 44, 55.
Foxholes, 7.
Fraisthorpe, 53.
Frenchgate, 59.
Fridaythorpe, 53.
Frizinghall, 17.
Frodingham, North &
    South, 26.
Fryston, Ferry, 17, 48.
Fryston, Monk, 17, 37.
Fryton, 54.
Fryup, 7.
Fulford, Gate, 26, 37.
Fulford, Water, 26, 37.
Full Sutton, v. Sutton, Full.
Fulstone, 28.
Fylingdales, 17, 26.

G

Gallowgate, 58.
Galphay, 25.
Galtres, 46.
Gammersgill, 48.
Ganthorpe, 53.
Ganton, 54.
Garforth, 49.
Gargrave, 49.
Garriston, 54.
Garrowby, 53.
Garsdale, 45.
Garton, 19.
Garton on the Wolds, 19.
Gateforth, 50.
Gate Fulford, v. Fulford,
    Gate.
Gate Helmsley, v. Helmsley,
    Gate.
Gatenby, 41.
Gayle, 45.
Gayles, 45.
Gembling, 17, 26.
Gibbet Street, 58.
Giggleswick, 28, 51.
Gildersome, 52.
Gilling, 17, 26, 51.
Gillygate, 58.
Gilmonby, 53.
Girsby, 53.
Gisburn, 32.
Givendale, Y.E., 30.
Givendale, Y.N., 30.
Givendale, Y.W., 26.
Glaisdale, 15.
Glass Houghton, v.
    Houghton, Glass.
Gledhow, 44.
Glusburn, 45.
Goathland, 51.
Golcar, 48.
Goldsborough, 27.
Gomersal, 27.
Goodmanham, 26.
Goodramgate, 59.
Goole, 55.
Gordale Scar, 60.
Gowdall, 24.
Gragareth, 44.
Gransmoor, 30.
Grantley, 28.
Grape Lane, 59.

Grassington, 19.
Greasebrough, 32.
Green Hammerton, v.
    Hammerton, Green.
Greetland, 24.
Greta, River, 42.
Grewelthorpe, 55.
Gribthorpe, 53.
Grimston, 54.
Grimston, Hanging, 37, 54.
Grimston, North, 54.
Grimthorpe, 53.
Grindale, 30.
Grindleton, 19.
Grinton, 19.
Gristhorpe, 53.
Grosmont, 55.
Guisborough, 54.
Guiseley, 23.
Gunnerside, 48.
Gunthwaite, 43.

H

Habton, Great & Little, 28.
Hack Fall, 60.
Hackforth, 26.
Hackness, 30.
Haddlesey, Chapel, 33.
Haddlesey, West, 33.
Haddock Stone, 60.
Haddockstones, 60.
Haigh, 25.
Haisthorpe, 53.
Haldenby, 53.
Hales, 24.
Halifax, 24.
Halikeld Wapentake, 45, 52.
Hallam, 45.
Hallamshire, 16.
Halsham, 45.
Haltemprice, 55.
Halton, 24.
Halton Gill, 24.
Halton, East & West, 24.
Hambleton, 29.
Hambleton (Selby), 29.
Hammerton, Green, 20.
Hammerton, Kirk, 20.
Hamphall Stubbs, v. Stubbs,
    Hamphall.
Hampole, 33.
Hampsthwaite, 43.
Handsworth, 28.
Hanging Grimston, v.
    Grimston, Hanging.
Hanging Royd, v. Royd,
    Hanging.
Hanlith, 45.
Hardcastle, 55.
Hardwick, East & West,
    21, 36.
Harewood, 31.
Harlow, 30.
Harlsey, East & West, 33.
Harlthorpe, 53.
Harmby, 53.
Harome, 35.
Harpham, 21.
Harrogate, 48.
Harswell, 32.
Harthill, 7.
Hartlington, 27.
Hartoft, 44.
Harton, 28.
Hartshead, 30.
Hartwith, 46.

Harwood Dale, 31.
Hatfield, 49.
Hatfield, Great & Little, 49.
Haugh, 24.
Haughs, 25.
Hauxwell, 32.
Havercroft, 22.
Hawes, 45.
Hawkswick, 54.
Hawksworth, 28.
Hawnby, 53.
Haworth, 25.
Hawsker, 47.
Haxby, 53.
Hayton, 19.
Hazlewood, 7, 50.
Headingley, 26.
Healaugh, 23.
Healey, 23.
Hebblethwaite, 43.
Hebden, 30.
Hebden Bridge, 30.
Heber's Ghyll, 60.
Heck, Great & Little, 26, 36.
Heckmondwike, 28.
Hedon, 29.
Hellifield, 54.
Helmsley, 28.
Helmsley, Gate, 28, 37.
Helmsley, Upper, 28.
Helperby, 53.
Helperthorpe, 53.
Helwith, 48.
Hemingbrough, 54.
Hemlington, 27.
Hempholme, 44.
Hemsworth, 28.
Hengate, 59.
Hensall, 54.
Heptonstall, 20.
Hepworth, 28.
Hesketh, 46.
Heslerton, East & West, 20.
Heslington, 20.
Hessay, 50.
Hessle, 50.
Hetton, 19.
Hewick, Bridge, 21, 37.
Hewick, Copt, 21, 37.
Heworth, 25.
Heyshaw, 25.
Hickleton, 19
Hiendley, South, 23.
High Street, 58.
Hildenley, 28.
Hilderthorpe, 53.
Hillam, 29.
Hilston, 54.
Hilton, 29.
Hinderskelfe, 51.
Hinderwell, 32.
Hipperholme, 35.
Hipswell, 32.
Hirst, 31.
Hirst Courtney, 31, 57.
Hirst, Temple, 31, 38.
Hodder, River, 10, 13.
Holbeck, 45.
Holderness, 52.
Hollym, 21.
Holme, 44.
Holme (Holmfirth), 31.
Holme upon Spalding
    Moor, 37.
Holmfirth, 31.
Holmpton, 44.
Holtby, 53.
Holwick, 45.

67

70

Place-Names outside Yorkshire

71